The Woman Who Saved An Island

The Woman Who Saved An Island

THE STORY OF SANDY WEST & OSSABAW ISLAND

by Jane Fishman

Real People Publishing

SAVANNAH, GEORGIA

The Woman Who Saved an Island—
The Story of Sandy West and Ossabaw Island
Second Edition
© 2014 by Jane Fishman

Published by Real People Publishing

All rights reserved. No part of this publication may be reproduced, stored in a retrieval system, or transmitted, in any form by any means, electronic, mechanical, photocopying, recording, or otherwise, without the prior written permission of the publisher.

If you would like to order more copies of *The Woman Who Saved an Island— The Story of Sandy West and Ossabaw Island*, go to Lulu.com and search under the book title or the author's name.

Book Design by Tom Greensfelder

ISBN 978-1-4951-3082-3

Printed in the United States of America

For Eleanor "Sandy" Torrey West

Chapter One

The Island

It's not easy getting to Ossabaw Island. You can't fly; there are no airports, there are no runways. You can't drive; there are no bridges. There is no ferry system. You wouldn't want to get into a boat with a novice. The tides are tricky. More than once I've seen people lodged on a sandbar in the Georgia bight, a curve of coastline from Cape Fear, North Carolina to Cape Canaveral, Florida. There they sit, high and dry and confused, waiting for the high tide to come in so they can motor on.

The island, which many people may have heard of but few have visited, is one of the most remote of Georgia's string of barrier islands. Tybee Island, connected to the mainland by a series of bridges that hardly seem like bridges, a playground for Savannah residents and visitors, sits to the north. But it hardly feels like an island. Another set of islands known as the Golden Isles hug the coast extending southward from Ossabaw: St. Catherines, Blackbeard, Sapelo, St. Simons and Jekyll. Finally, there's Cumberland, a spit away from Florida's Amelia Island.

If you take a boat and pull it up on to Ossabaw's beach, you would not be able to spend the night. Ossabaw, twenty miles south of Savannah, belongs to the state of Georgia. No one is allowed to step past the high tide mark. To visit, you have to obtain permission from the Ossabaw Island Foundation, a nonprofit group that acts as an extension of the state. The Foundation does offer opportunities for writing, birding, artistic, sci-

The island is still wild and unchanged.

entific, archeological groups, but only after you apply. Recreation activities that don't include research, study and education are prohibited.

I have visited as a newspaper reporter, an artist, a participant in the yearly Pig Roast and Art Show (a fundraiser for the Ossabaw Island Foundation), and, most recently, as a friend of Eleanor "Sandy" Torrey West. Sandy inherited the island from her parents, who bought it in 1924. In 1978 when she could no longer handle the escalating taxes, she negotiated a "bargain" sale to the state of Georgia. She never once entertained the idea of selling it and watching someone turn a bit of paradise into a commercial and populated Hilton Head Island. Dealing with the state was a challenge. There were plenty of hoops to navigate, caveats to negotiate, personalities to sooth, conditions as convoluted and serpentine as the Spanish moss dangling from Ossabaw's sprawling live oak trees. She wanted only one thing—to ensure the island's wild and wonderful nature. She held her ground. Now she has a set of ironclad restrictions and a lifetime estate to live on the island and in the house. Sandy West is 101 years old.

The island is still wild and unchanged. The house still stands though few of the doors lock and it's not unusual to seek a skink in the kitchen or an opossum in the long downstairs hall. Winter nights can be dark, summer afternoons steamy and endless, mornings crisp and glorious. There are window units that provide heat and air but no central air conditioning. A full moon sends dramatic beams onto the water and lights up the front lawn. Since the house faces east, there is no more beautiful sunrise. After a few days in the house a routine sets in. When you wake up and walk downstairs to make coffee you're apt to look out the kitchen window and see three or four deer, skittish, alert; a half dozen pigs rooting around; a dark and massive hog, and a couple of slow and lumbering donkeys, all coexisting, all sharing the same space. Until the end of 2013 when she died, Poco, Sandy's 30-year-old horse, would have been amongst them, eating grass, looking graceful, fitting in. As before, the number of four-legged creatures far outnumber the two-legged variety.

But back to the dock: when you step off the boat and regain your land legs, you walk up the ramp (which can be quite steep if you arrive at low tide), load your gear in the back of a waiting truck—often left with the key in the ignition—and drive to the main house, where you leave the vehicle (key in place). Or you could choose to walk the mile on a sandy, agreeable road past cabbage palms, sable and sawtooth palmettos, pools of water, egrets and the occasional single blue heron. The island's interior is home to wood storks and loggerhead sea turtles. The trail is shady and, often, depending on the weather, strewn with palm fronds. You may hear a rustle in the marsh, turn quickly and see the pink ears of an armadillo scurry under the brush. You may see a rattler crossing the road. If it's a hot day you could spot an alligator sunning off to the side. You may pass a truck from a handful of Department of Natural Resources personnel who work during the day on the island or the fulltime pig hunter. Most likely you will have the road to yourself.

There are no trashcans, real estate offices, orange traffic cones, billboards, signposts or corner stores to buy provisions.

While the island grows wilder, the house never seems to change. There was a serious roof leak a few years ago that the Ossabaw Island Foundation addressed with a new roof. There is water damage in some of the rooms and hallways. There is some sign of termite damage, but you have to look closely to see it. The floor joists are so strong you don't hear a single squeak when you walk up either set of stairs—both have landings—or down the long, dark hallways. Inside, bookshelves crowded with first editions from people who spent time at the esteemed Ossabaw Island Project are tucked into every corner. The antique rugs, worn with soft warm colors, while a tad thinner, don't change.

The house is welcoming.

Elizabeth Gray Vining, a guest at the Ossabaw Island Project who came to work on her book, *Being Seventy, The Measure of a Year*, described Ossabaw this way: "Eleanor's theory is that the house is like a fairy tale, on an island hung with moss and magic, separated from ordinary life by the miles of sea; that the mind goes back to childhood when fairy tales were real, and that hidden and submerged dreams and fears come to the surface again."

Tabby cabins.

About Sandy West, Vining writes, "Gallant Eleanor is like a modern Canute bidding the waves roll back and everywhere the ghosts are waiting… Eleanor West, a vital, even a glowing, person, sat at the head of the table and kept the conversation moving."

Vining was a former private tutor to Crown Prince Akihito, the heir apparent of the Imperial House of Japan between 1946 and 1952.

Most of the time it's people—human beings—who change the natural order of things. On Ossabaw, maybe because there were so few human beings who "owned" the island or, more recently, maybe because Sandy sold it to the state with ironclad restrictions, the order has remained constant. If someone who visited in the twenties or the thirties were to magically drop in today, he or she would find very little that has changed. The nine and a half miles of beach—except for some erosion—look the same. The three pre-Civil War tabby cabins, built of oyster shells, lime, sand and water for African-Americans during slavery, look—thanks to major renovation work—much as they did one hundred fifty years ago. For eighty years Sandy West's family farmed, timbered, hunted and planted trees. In 1961, she and her then husband Clifford West shifted the focus toward the cultural.

With any luck and an army of vigilant Sandy-trained watchdogs, the Ossabaw Island Foundation will see that nothing on Ossabaw changes. But it won't be without Sandy's constant reminder: "Humans are so mettlesome," she likes to say. "They just can't leave things alone."

Chapter Two

The Woman Who Saved an Island

I did not know Eleanor Ford Torrey West as the blonde, curly-headed child of privilege who grew up in a grand Beaux-Arts mansion called Clairview in Grosse Pointe, Michigan. Nor did I know her as the ten-year-old who wintered with her family in a forty-room Georgian style mansion called Greenwich in Savannah, Georgia.

I did not know Eleanor the debutante, when she was introduced to "polite society;" Eleanor the finishing-school student at The Masters School in Dobbs Ferry, New York, or Eleanor, the bride who wore her mother's gown when she got married in Michigan at Grosse Pointe Memorial Church with a reception at Clairview, the same gown her daughter would wear decades later, the mark of a sentimental, old-world family.

In truth, I did not know her as Eleanor. When we met she was Sandy.

I never met either of her husbands, John Shallcross or Clifford West.

I never met the horsewoman who knew so well the cabbage palm-lined trails of Ossabaw Island she could probably ride them blindfolded, or the dabbler-in-the-metaphysical who in 1972 received a diploma from Witch Gundella certifying her as a witch's apprentice.

I did not know her pet pigs Maria Bosomworth, Oglethorpe, Musgrove, Pulaski, Lucky or Sassoon. Nor did I ever see them walk through the Spanish-style main house on Ossabaw. I did not know a gray donkey named Mr. Pip; the goose named Christmas; dogs Jonesie, William Rodgers and Muzza Kunk (the nickname of a child-

S
he spends many hours on what she calls her "thinking tour."

Jane, Sandy and Toby.

hood friend, Mary Katherine Reynolds); Sultan, the Brahmin bull, or the peahen that learned to tap on the door to ask for Saltines. I did know the pig, Paul Mitchell ("He had a hair problem").

I did know her horse Poco and her dog, Toby, aka Tobias, Toby Tyler or Toby Tinctum. Both have since passed away, Poco in 2013, Toby in 2014.

I did not camp out, grow vegetables, milk cows or raise chickens at Middle Place, the plantation turned interdisciplinary colony that overlooks Buckhead Creek, part of the tidal marsh facing the mainland. This experiment in living, known as the Genesis Project, ran from 1970 to 1982. This is where Sandy and her husband Clifford West, who taught sculpture at Cranbrook School of Art in Bloomfield Hills, Michigan, and had begun a career in innovative film-making, invited mostly college students to the barrier island to live off the grid, grow their own food, draw their own water from an artesian well and sleep in tree houses they built from lumber they harvested themselves.

Nor did I sit down at the twenty-four seat dining table at the main house on Ossabaw to eat dinner with fellow artists, writers, philosophers, mathematicians and linguists, a brilliant collection of people, who were there as part of the Ossabaw Island Project, another cutting-edge venture Sandy and Clifford offered.

I did not take part in any of the negotiations, consultations or discussions about how to deliver a gem known as Ossabaw to the state of Georgia in exchange for keeping the barrier island pristine and free of development, and offering a lifetime living arrangement for Sandy in the two-story house her parents built in 1926.

Except for Sandy's youngest child, Justin West, I never met any of her three other children, Michael, John or Gilian. Nor did I ever meet Betty Pool, Sandy's partner in travel and imagination (and her sister-in-law from her first husband, John Shallcross, who was the father of her three oldest children) with whom she wrote, *The God of the Hinge: Sojourns in Cloud Cuckoo Land, the story of Herme*s.

I met Sandy West in 2002 when she was eighty-nine through the unique and brilliant Jim Bitler, a crony of Sandy's and an old friend of mine. Jim was one of my first friends when I moved to Savannah as a newspaper reporter in the late 1980s. Jim was leading tours for Wilderness Southeast, a non-profit group that introduced newbies such as myself to the beauty and mystery of the Georgia Coast.

In 2003, Jim became the on-island Ossabaw Island Foundation coordinator, where he worked until his untimely death in 2011. It was and is exhilarating to cross the Ossabaw Sound in a motorboat, to see and smell the slightly sulfurous, shiny brown mud marsh known as pluff mud, to step onto the simple dock where two or three boats may be moored, rarely more.

But it was the island's doyenne who won my heart. When Jim took me over to the house to meet Sandy, who moved to Ossabaw fulltime in 1987, I spotted an animated woman on the short side with great posture and a mischievous smile. She was dressed in comfortable jeans, a little ragged at the bottom, a T-shirt, a pair of well-worn, faded blue Keds and bright socks. She was unpretentious and prone to making fun of the fancy, the "re-FINE," she would call them, the "i" in fine pronounced as a long "e," her tapered and well-manicured pinky sticking straight up as she exaggerated the word.

She could entertain for hours.

This was not what I expected. I knew Sandy as a mythic figure—a crusader of sorts. I also knew she came from Grosse Pointe, an exclusive, upper-class suburb, well known to anyone who lived near Detroit. This interested me since I too was from a Detroit suburb. Huntington Woods, while comfortable, was not nearly as wealthy or exclusive. Another difference between the two was that while Jews, such as myself, could live in Huntington Woods, we could not live in Grosse Pointe. That may not be true now but in the 1950s it was one of those "facts" everyone knew, particularly if you were Jewish.

I was spending a few days on Ossabaw as part of a group of artists who came to paint and draw. With great trepidation—the house is brimming with artwork by people such as sculptor Harry Bertoia, printmaker and photographer John McWilliams, photographer Jack Leigh and painters Craig Rubadoux and Yiannis Spyropoulos—I went to the main house with the other artists and handed over a picture I had painted.

"It's a thistle," Sandy said in her distinctive and dramatic voice, not unlike Julia Child's. "I have never before seen anyone paint a thistle." She seemed to like it. She thought it so "worthwhile"—a favorite word of hers, then and now—she hung it above one of the two deep sinks in her kitchen. It's still there.

After that initial meeting we would spend many, many hours together. At first I visited with organized groups of artists from Georgia. After that, with Sandy's permission, I would schedule a visit and follow up the trip with a column published in the Savannah Morning News, where I worked fulltime for twenty years and now on a freelance basis. With my sketchpad at hand, I would draw her or draw items in the house. We would share meals. I would cook although Sandy liked being there to chop vegetables, provide commentary and set the table.

I loved her spunk, her curiosity, her quickness and her interest in other people. Well into her one-hundredth year, surrounded by eight people and four dogs, I heard her say, "I just love people who love one another." But it was her humor and

Thistle painting by Jane Fishman hanging in Sandy's kitchen.

her choice of language I loved best. The stories were infectious, sometimes made-up, always expressive. They did not end. This was a woman who did not seem aware of her age.

Some days she'd be feeling "crisp," some days not. If she was expecting visitors, a "big punkin," for instance, a phrase I would hear often, maybe someone from a national historic trust organization or a possible donor to the Ossabaw Island Foundation, she'd have to "tizzy-up" the house and prepare to get "tittie nice."

She'd have to "pee-rooz," as in peruse or search, for her glasses (or dentures). But it was always, "Good morning, sweet pea" and "Thank you, lovie."

She was quick, even the time she was in the hospital fighting bronchitis.

"Do you drink?" a nurse asked, reading from a list of perfunctory questions without really expecting or listening for an honest answer.

"With pleasure," Sandy answered, without missing a beat.

Sandy was entertaining, challenging, thoughtful and feisty. She was a real pistol. I'd never met anyone like her. None of that has changed. In the last twelve years, we have spent many days sprawled on her bed, which doubles as her desk, in a sunny second-floor bedroom (no moving downstairs for her) that measures 16-by-18-feet. Always flexible, she sits ramrod straight, legs crossed, lotus-style. She has no television, no radio. There's no sign of any newspapers. Except for *Time* magazine, she does not read periodicals. She has always loved books; they surround her still. She has a busy correspondence. She loves the birds at the birdfeeder but unlike myself or other people worried about their memory she does not fret if she can't remember what kind they are.

"Do you care what they're called?" she asked. "I don't. They don't care what they're called. Why should I? That's the kind of memory I have. The only other person I've read about like this is Carl Jung. He said he couldn't remember anything from the outside, only from the inside. I can remember how I felt certain days, but I have no memory of dates. Nor do I care about them."

She spends many hours on what she calls her "thinking tour." For years, she likes to say, before someone invented the wheel or mastered fire, no one had a clue about either of these things.

"I keep hoping for another 'pop-in'," she said once, using her term for an idea.

Her needs are simple. When I plan to visit and ask what she wants, her grocery list includes celery, garlic, leaf lettuce, cottage cheese (large curd), eggs, butter, bananas, white wine, good bread for her and old bread for the raccoons.

I have never known her to be bored.

First thing in the morning and last thing at night she pries up the window near the small refrigerator in her bedroom, pushes open the screen and tosses bread and kitchen scraps to her beloved donkeys, pigs, the occasional peacock and, most recently, an opossum that has taken to climbing up the outside walls of the house. She makes her way down the long upstairs hall lined with framed photographs that include Greg Allman and President Jimmy Carter to a computer her son Justin set up for her. Not long after complaining about which key to "poke," she caught on.

She walks carefully and with purpose. With a series of strategically positioned walkers situated on the top and the bottom of two steps on the second floor—two levels that delineated the bedrooms for the family and guests and the bedrooms for the "help"—and at the bottom of a second set of stairs leading to the kitchen, she navigates her way at dinnertime to share a meal with whomever is visiting. The meal always includes "a nip," a glass or two of white wine. Either before or after dinner she might maneuver her walker down the long hall to the outside door to hand-feed the deer or, before he died, visit her thirty-year-old horse, Poco. She's always up for a drive to areas on Ossabaw—Middle Place, Bradley Beach or Cabbage Gardens. As the driver on many of these excursions, I worry about losing our way in the island's nine thousand acres, about encountering an armadillo in the middle of the road, about driving too close to a tidal creek and edging into the water or waiting for an eight-foot alligator to make it to the other side, about getting back home before dark. She does not.

She does not obsess about the past. Nor does she romanticize the past.

She does worry about the future of the island, which since 1978—when she could no longer afford the taxes—has been under the auspices of the state of Georgia.

She wants what she's always wanted: to keep the island wild and undeveloped. She wants people to use Ossabaw the way it was stipulated in her original agreement with the state—for cultural, scientific and/or educational purposes. She does not want it bulldozed and turned into a resort culture. But she doesn't want it kept like

Island artifacts.

a museum, either. She wants people to experience its tranquility and mystery. She does not want recreational activity to become the main focus.

Andy Meadows, who works for the Georgia Department of Natural Resources and has spent years on Ossabaw, agrees. "I've seen a lot of Hilton Head Islands," he says, "and I know for a fact Ossabaw could have been one of them without Mrs. West."

In our time together I have seen her spitting angry at how the state hasn't maintained the island's roads or the causeway as promised, how the cellular age and accompanying cellular towers have interfered with the true and original definition of a remote island, how the "big punkins" just don't get what nature has to offer. I have heard her talk of "people," only to realize she is talking, quite deliberately, quite consciously, of animals. I have questioned some of her stories from seventy to eighty years ago—names of cars she drove, well-known people she entertained or characters such as sports writer Grantland Rice, who visited to make a short film about duck hunting—only to Google the names and to see she was right on. There are many things I haven't been able to pin down. But like Sandy's attitude about not fretting if she can't remember the names of the birds that feast outside her window, I'm going to record only what I do know, only what I have seen.

She could have used this time of her life to kick back, to take it easy. But that is not Sandy. She likes company, she cares deeply about people, she loves Ossabaw. When an old friend telephones, she's apt to say, "Sweetie, the island is waiting for you to make a visit." She is a thinker, a searcher. She likes the process of looking for new ideas and watching them germinate. She likes to gather disparate elements, throw them into a pot and see what happens. For the Ossabaw Island Project, she and her husband Clifford West could have just invited writers or painters to the island the way other artist retreats have done. But they had a different approach. They chose to invite thousands of philosophers, mathematicians, linguists, musicians AND artists to see what kind of stew they could cook up.

That cost money, of course. Between 1961 and 1982, Sandy has said, they probably spent half a million dollars annually. Some of that money came after her mother's death in 1959, some of it from the sale of Ossabaw to the state. Some people in her family thought she was crazy for holding on to the island. They thought she was foolish not to sell to developers for big bucks, such as Charles Fraser, who created Hilton Head Island, now a resort town in South Carolina. Or even Jackie and Aristotle Onassis, who expressed interest. Today there are others who think she is a bit daft for not vacating the island and spending the rest of her life in what they regard as a more comfortable and safe existence on the mainland.

Just recently I found a children's book Sandy wrote and illustrated with her own photographs, *Maria Bosomworth and William Rodgers*, which the Beehive Press printed and published in a limited edition in 1976. The book is a touching story about a pig, Maria, and a dog, William, although much of it could be used to describe Sandy.

"As Maria grew older and did not spend as much time eating and sleeping, she began to think about people and wonder why most of them rushed about so much of the time.

"She supposed they were looking for warmth, comfort and love, too, but they searched in machines and seemed to be too busy to look in the right places.

"Maria soon came to realize that there are two kinds of people:

THE PEOPLE-WHO-GO-BY

and

THE PEOPLE-WHO-STOP"

Sandy West is a person who stops: For a human being, for a four-legged animal, for a new idea. For an island. This book, *The Woman Who Saved an Island*, which uses Sandy's words as much as possible, is about that person—not her husbands, not her children, not her money. Those are not my concerns. This story is about someone raised in wealth who has chosen to spend her fortune and final years keeping a place wild and untamed and free of strip malls, tiki bars, chain restaurants and nail parlors. It's a look at and a love story of an uncommon, fierce, straight-talking, brave woman.

Chapter Three

In The Beginning

Eleanor Torrey West came from another era. Her people bought islands. They went on safaris. They entertained on yachts. They gave weeklong parties. People such as her mother, Nell Ford Torrey, had tweenys (definition: noun, archaic, informal for maids), people who made sure her pocketbook held a hanky, a compact, a teeny bottle of sherry and perhaps a supply of ammonia ampoule or smelling salts before she set off in the back seat of her chauffeur's car for a shopping visit in downtown Detroit.

"Can you imagine?" Sandy asks, using one of her favorite phrases. "Mother would drive downtown in her Lincoln limousine and people would wave at her. They knew that along with the tremendous wealth came the orchestra, the art museum, the symphony. Can you imagine? I was brought up to give. I was told I should give to other people."

The family kept a Model T station wagon in Quebec, where they went in the summer.

"At home, Mother had a Pierce-Arrow, father a coupe. In Grosse Pointe, the garage had one of those turn-around things that sat in the middle of the driveway, something one of our drivers could move manually. It would bring up whatever vehicle they wanted," Sandy said.

Later, when Sandy's parents moved to Ossabaw to escape Michigan winters her mother, Nell, who was named after her sister Stell's favorite doll, would bring her new 1926 Packard along with a chauffeur.

I was brought up to give.

The Torrey-West house on Ossabaw Island.

"We had a squash court. Does anyone play squash anymore? We had a man-made lake at the end of our playhouse. We would spend nights there," Sandy said. "We had an elevator as big as my bathroom. I'd keep my chewing gum there, Wrigley's."

Sandy's maternal great-grandfather, John Baptiste Ford, was a brilliant and daring entrepreneur who started the Pittsburgh Plate Glass Company. Her mother donated a painting—the "Cottage Madonna" by nineteenth-century Dutch artist Jozef Israels—to the Detroit Institute of Arts. Her father, Henry Norton Torrey, a physician, served in World War I. He came from the rolling hills of Creston, Iowa, in the southwestern part of the state. Nell met Dr. Torrey through her mother, Ella Neat Ford, who was one of Torrey's patients.

The original wall telephone.

"Dad was an ambidextrous surgeon on the battlefield," Sandy said. "He had a big brain, a busy mind. Mother's people were big punkins, not Dad's. Mother was a parasol lady."

In Grosse Pointe, the family lived on Lake Shore Road in a grand house at the time when houses had grand names, along with vast lawns, lavish gardens, huge old elms and spreading maples. Part of the Torrey property was the location of "Claireview," a Jersey stock farm owned by George S. Davis, a partner in the pharmaceutical company, Parke-Davis.

Two of Sandy's aunts had houses on the same street. Aunt Stell Schlotman's house was called

Stonehurst. Aunt Hester Speck lived in Fairholme. Sandy's grandfather, Emory L. Ford, had one of the largest mansions on Lake Shore. It was referred to as the Emory L. Ford Mansion. Edsel Ford, Henry Ford's son and no relation to Nell, lived close by. Her great-grandfather, John Baptiste Ford, built the MacNichol House, now the home of the Wyandotte Historical Museum in Wyandotte, Michigan. A painting of this house with the horse and carriage in front hangs in Sandy's house.

Nell and Henry's house was built in 1913, the year Sandy was born.

"Our chauffeur had a house," she said. "The gardener had a house. We had cows. We'd go milk them. Imagine, in Grosse Pointe, Michigan. We had a huge garden, with chickens. Can you beat that? Of course, I took it all for granted."

When the endless upkeep and escalating taxes on the houses, built in the early twentieth-century and designed by such architects as Albert Kahn, Albert Spahr, and John Scott, became too much, they were torn down. The land was subdivided. In at least one instance, in the late nineteen-sixties, thirty-eight houses replaced one mansion.

After Sandy's parents bought Ossabaw in 1924, a mesmerizing place of maritime live oak forests, salt marshes and feral pigs, where you can walk for hours on the undulating stretch of beach and not see another human being, and built a house on it in 1926, "a barge brought Dad's coupe (and chauffeur) and mother's Lincoln or maybe it was the Packard. I don't remember. The chauffeur drove down with mother's parrot in a cage."

For entertainment the Torreys had the company of the other northern industrialists who also owned islands and boats.

"Once Dick Reynolds sent his big yacht, The Sapelo, for us," Sandy remembered, speaking of R.J. Reynolds, Jr., the tobacco giant who bought Sapelo Island, another barrier island off Georgia, in 1933.

"We drank champagne at every stop on our way to Sapelo and shot skeet and went into little houses to check our lipstick and freshen our hair. Then we went to our rooms to dress for dinner. There was a closet of bathing suits to choose from. We'd wait for a knock on the door for a massage and then go down later to dinner and dance to a black orchestra."

Sandy likes to say she always lived near water. From her upstairs bedroom in the family's Grosse Pointe mansion on Lake Shore Road, she could see Lake St. Clair and the coast of Canada. From Greenwich, the turn-of-the-century mansion in Savannah that her family wintered in—the one that burned when Sandy was ten—the family could see the Wilmington River. The house on Ossabaw Island faces Ossabaw Sound, which leads to the Atlantic Ocean.

She shakes her head thinking of how her family lived.

"Dad belonged to a chi-chi trout fishing club in northern Michigan," she says, although when I asked what that meant she said she wasn't sure.

"Mother didn't do a lick," Sandy muses. "But she was always busy. She did a lot of poor people things, you know, helping out and such. And she played bridge and canasta. And she tipped tables. Did you ever do that? You sit down at a table, put your hands on it and say, 'Is anyone there?' Mother and her friends did it like mad fiends. Isn't that the last straw? She'd say, 'Have you got a message? Is there a message for Sandy?' You'd go through the alphabet. They were very serious.

Eleanor Ford Torrey towel in the bathroom.
Right: Sandy's parents, Nell and Henry.

"We used to tip tables all the time, like if we wanted to do something. I haven't done it for a long time. We had a table in Michigan I remember, me and the daughter of the captain of our boat. Once, the table started moving. You won't believe it. We were in the living room. It pulled us out of the room and, lovie, the table took steps. It went upstairs to the second floor. I'm not telling you a lie. The stairs were carpeted and it went up step by step. We never could have pushed it up. I tried it here but it didn't work."

That didn't faze Sandy.

"There's so much in the universe we don't know and scoff at," she says.

The family was friendly with Howard Coffin, an automotive engineer with the Hudson Motor Company in Detroit, credited with building the first internal combustion engine. He was a millionaire by age thirty. Coffin, who first came to Savannah in the early twentieth century to attend the International Road Races, bought nearby Sapelo Island in 1912 (except for the land owned by former slaves) and was part owner with two other people of

St. Catherines Island, which sits to the south. Coffin's love and knowledge of the Georgia Sea Islands is how Sandy's parents got to the coast in the first place.

Coffin's wife was Sandy's godmother.

"One day he told me he wanted to build me a car," Sandy said of Coffin. "I was just a teenager but I told him I wanted a roadster with a pointed back. And I wanted it to be half-yellow and half-red. Can you imagine anything more hideous? But he built it. I drove all around Grosse Pointe for years. It was that kind of life. But we never got snooty. Why would we? Everyone else was like us."

When Sandy's family bought Ossabaw Island, it was not unusual for people such as the Torreys to buy and sell barrier islands. The Carnegies, whose business was steel, once owned most of nearby Cumberland Island when Andrew Carnegie's younger brother, Thomas, purchased the island in 1881.

Philip Berolzheimer, whose father, Daniel, started the Eagle Pencil Company, bought nearby Little St. Simons Island in 1908. His descendants own part of it today with former U.S. Treasury Secretary, Henry Paulson, and his wife, Wendy.

Ossabaw's previous owners, members of the Savannah Steamship Company that used it for hunting, approached the Torreys many times to buy the heart-shaped island. The Michigan family always turned them down. Up until then all they knew was Grosse Pointe and private yachts and Greenwich. But the men from the club kept at it. When Nell had asked Henry, who was about to go out of town, what she should do about their persistence her husband counseled, "Offer the man $150,000 and he'll leave you alone." So that's what she did. Except to her surprise the club accepted the offer.

For the Torreys, the timing was perfect. Greenwich had burned down. The family, who had been living on their yacht in the Wilmington River, had sold the land to the city of Savannah for Forest Lawn Cemetery. And, because of Nell's legendary grandfather, John Baptiste Ford, the Torreys were flush with money. In today's terms, $150,000 would be slightly more than two million dollars.

In the end, it was this man, her great-grandfather, who became such a looming presence in Sandy's life. When pressed with astronomical taxes on the island, dissenting opinions from her late brother's children, and big decisions about what to do with Ossabaw, it was this distant relative, someone she never met, who "offered" guidance.

"He was a total genius," Sandy likes to say. "Every time I go by his portrait in the house I hear him saying, 'Look, I was 87 when I started the Michigan Alkali Company in Wyandotte.'"

Then, still looking at his oil painting, she imagines him saying to her, "This is no time to rest. Get off your butt and do something."

And so she did. She saved an island.

Chapter Four

Transformation

"It's so funny," Sandy said one morning from her bed, removing one of her many pairs of glasses to punctuate the thought. "People think I'm rich. They think I'm a grand heiress. And that's so not true."

At least not anymore.

She had just hung up from a conversation with her son, Justin, who had called from Morocco ("Can you imagine?"), where he was on sabbatical. They were talking about bank accounts, doctors' bills, the constant house maintenance and other financial matters, all things that needed tending from afar.

"I used to have money but not now," she said, putting down the receiver of her trusty landline that broadcasts in large letters the date, time and number of who is calling. "But no one has a retirement home like mine."

Between the Ossabaw Island Project (1961 to 1980) *and* the Genesis Project (1970 to 1982), Sandy figures she spent between $800,000 and one million dollars a year, in today's dollars.

While her mother and father spent buckets of money on butlers, upstairs and downstairs maids, servants, tutors, laundresses, chauffeurs, boat captains, barge drivers, portrait artists, cattlemen and cooks, Sandy had other ideas for her resources. But the cost of transporting, feeding and maintaining the vehicles and the facilities for artists, writers and philosophers to Ossabaw would add up.

Sandy already knew about affluence and privilege, about fine silver and proper table settings. But by the

No one has a retirement home like mine.

Torrey-West house.

Sandy with Justin's t-shirt.

time she was ten, when she, her parents and her brother Bill started spending winters at Ossabaw, escaping the Michigan climate, she started to learn about nature. She started to live in nature, a visceral experience she never forgot. She may have been alone with silence for the first time in her life. She learned to cope with danger or, as she says, "with rumrunners, poachers, real serpents, all the things people try to invent."

It took a while to shed her upbringing, her exalted upper-class mores, the social class she was born into, the comfort she had come to expect. It's not a transition that occurs overnight. More than once she has looked at something—maybe her dog Toby on her bed or the T-shirts she has come to love wearing (her latest favorite, sent by Justin, reads, "Life is a Ho-Ax")—and said, "Mother would have a cow if she could see this."

She often talked of her time on the island with her brother, who was two years older. "We each had our own tutor. They came to the island with us and stayed from January to May. Following breakfast, Bill and I were to head upstairs for our studies. I remember on more than one occasion going up the stairs in the living room only to scoot secretly down the back stairs to sneak out the back door to run out and explore and play on the island. I learned so much by being outside. So much more than I could learn out of books. I mean I know how to change a tire."

Before moving to Ossabaw she and Bill would spend winters in the family's house on the Wilmington River. Even there Sandy and her brother managed to scare up adventure. The following one happened months after the house burned down (on Bill's birthday):

"We were all out there mucking around, looking for some of mother's jewelry, sometime after the ashes cooled off," Sandy said. "They found most of it, using a big sifter. But Bill and I found mother's engagement ring. We had picked up a huge hunk of glass. It had been on her dresser and when the mirror fell off the ring melted into the mirror."

Sandy remembers sitting at the main gate to the house—which had a sign that read, "Guests welcome, unwanted people not"—and making up stories for all the gawkers who would drive by the brick mansion. Unlike her house in Grosse Pointe, Greenwich, the site where Count Casimir Pulaski allegedly died in 1779, stood out. So did their lifestyle. In this neck of the woods, there were not other people like herself.

As a young woman Sandy, who married her second husband, Clifford West in 1952, traveled to Europe, perhaps befitting her class or because that's who she and her husband were. She lived in Italy and France for long periods of time. She learned to appreciate Old World values. When she returned to Ossabaw she brought with her an expanded mind and the germ of an idea for the future. She was happy to be home and she was ready for a change. Maybe without knowing it, she had missed the familiarity of the rattling palm fronds at night, the braying donkeys in the morning, the surrounding silence or the shadows of the yaupon holly, after which, some say, the island was named.

Maybe she missed being able to walk for miles through the maritime live oak forests and along the edges of its marshes without seeing another human being.

Maybe she missed the pig that would follow her around and into her house or the late-afternoon canary yellow glow on the tidal marshes. And when she had a chance—maybe after her mother died in 1959 and she had more money and she felt freer to follow her own dreams or maybe after her children were living their own lives—she realized these were things she wanted to share with others.

In 1961, she and West launched a project that would bring together all kinds of people to a place of reverence she believed in, to her island, to Ossabaw. They had the idea that mixing up the disciplines—having a linguist talk to a poet about words or a painter look at the stars with an astronomer or a geologist dissect a word in Latin with a translator—could only enhance what they were working on.

So instead of supervising a Downton Abbey-type house staff along with maintaining proper fine china and beautiful stemware for the upstairs half of the population, Sandy spent her money and offered up her island to the creative, intellectual class.

Later, on the cusp of the environmental awareness movement, she came up with the Genesis Project, another innovative way to introduce people to nature. She would put everything she had towards keeping the island wild and whole.

Once, contemplating the future of Ossabaw, the specter of escalating taxes and the pressure from others to develop it, she wrote,

> *This is terribly, terribly scary, but it is also challenging and get-at-able. For one thing is sure, and that is if yesterday's solutions simply do not fit today's problems someone will jolly well have to think up some new ideas, and in this untouched field my guess is as good as yours. We think it is really terrific to say, "I don't know anything more. I don't know whom to rely on any more." I cannot even find words in our language that will explain clearly what might be done.*
>
> *And so I am not going to keep on trying to make old ways fit into this new world, nor am I going to give up— I am just going to admit that I know nothing and I am going to start from scratch.*

While sitting one day in her kitchen, which still sports a handsome if worn black-and-white tile floor, a built-in cabinet and the bones of an old-fashioned wooden icebox, I found among the stacks of books and old calendars of magnificent Grosse Pointe houses that have met the wrecking ball an overflowing scrapbook from the Ossabaw Island Project. Each Project member signed the book and added their identifying interest:

writer, folk singer, bottle collector, textile designer, astronomer, automobile executive stylist, literary critic, historian, sociologist, playwright, beachcomber, biographer, philosopher, dentist, archeologist, printmaker, ornithologist (in theory), museum curator, botanical illustrator, anthropologist, paleontologist, poet, geologist, physicist, microbiologist, pygmy expert, Shakespearian expert, Medieval lyric poet, songwriter, musicologist, mathematician, ethno mycologist, storyteller, historical archeologist, farmer, environmental sculptor, yoga therapist, double bassist, lepidopterist, zoologist, ecologist, amanueusist, evangelist, biologist and theologian.

Participants came from all parts of the United States as well as Norway, Mexico, Israel, France, New Zealand, Holland and South Africa.

Some of the authors included Margaret Atwood, Annie Dillard, Arthur Imerti, Rose Rappoport Moss, Menakhem Perry, Olive Ann Burns and Ralph Ellison. Translator Willard Trask was there, along with linguist and literary theorist Roman Jakobson. There were painters Lamar Dodd, Leigh Hyams, Ora Lerman and Jean Zaleski, and photographers John Earl and Nancy Marshall. There was composer Aaron Copeland (who participated as a

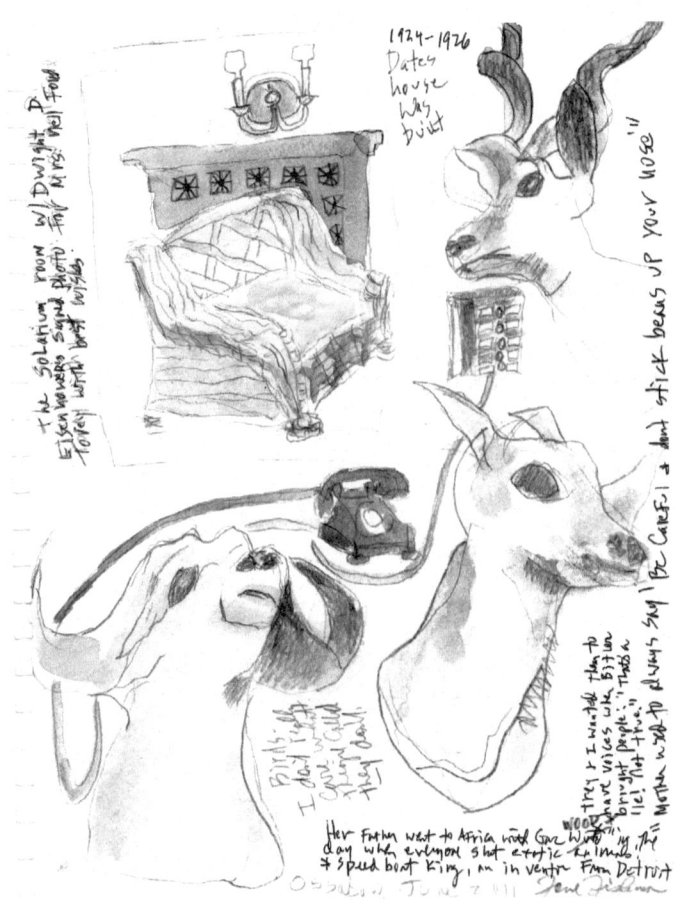

A page from Jane's sketchbook.

board member), conductor Samuel Barber and Italian sculptor Harry Bertoia. There was Marshall Fredericks, a sculptor who created the "Spirit of Detroit" statue in Detroit.

"Don't forget the dressmaker from New Zealand," Sandy said. "She ending up writing a book called, 'Suit Yourself.'"

For the project Sandy housed and fed the visitors in the 1926 house her parents built. It has sixteen bedrooms and fifteen baths. For her own privacy (and probably sanity, as she has expressed more than once), she moved to the boarding house, a century-old dwelling about a mile from the mansion. It had been shipped in pieces to Ossabaw by department store tycoon John Wanamaker of Philadelphia. It was a two-story prefabricated house that had been touted at the Philadelphia Centennial Exposition of 1876 as the latest thing in the building trade.

"For the project we invited all those people here and didn't tell them what it was for," Sandy said to me one night when we were having a nip of white wine and a first course of celery stuffed with hummus in the kitchen before dinner, her beagle, Toby, sprawled on the floor. "For three days we watched their interactions. Just like we thought, the artist didn't talk to other artists but to scientists and musicians and writers, which was exactly what we were hoping would happen.

"This is what we were after. One day I was standing in the kitchen when I heard two people coming in from the beach. They were arguing. I heard one say, 'I can't wait to show her what we found.' The other said, 'You said I could tell her.' Then the first said, 'No, I'm going to.'

"They had turned into children. Between the beach, the woods, the wildlife, they were not the same as when they came. Just think of them all sitting around the dining room table. Can you imagine?"

The hard thing today would be to imagine people sitting around a dining room table and talking uninterrupted without frequent and sometimes surreptitious glances at individual cell phones either hidden on their laps or sitting out in the open.

But that's Ossabaw—challenging—even for a group of adventure-seeking, nature-loving, artist-types who had signed up for the Genesis Project. In 2010, eight of these people gathered for a reunion to talk about their experience off the grid, away from the mainland. The late historian Mark Findlay facilitated this discussion. Findlay was writing a book about Ossabaw at the time of his death in 2013.

"I was a city girl," said one of the participants. "They warned us about the bugs and the snakes but you weren't used to it visually or spiritually. You weren't prepared to fall in love with the place."

This same woman also remembered going to the mainland for provisions and being shocked at all the food in the grocery stores. It was so organized, she said.

"We thought we were going to save the world," said one of the other participants. "When I was there it was the first year of Earth Day. That was very much in our consciousness."

For another Genesis veteran, Ossabaw " informed the rest of my life."

And that, thanks to Sandy West, is what Ossabaw continues to do. It informs our lives.

Chapter Five

Nell and the House

If Sandy loved and fought for the island, her mother, Nell Ford Torrey, loved and developed the house.

If Sandy loved the animals, her mother loved the gardens.

If Sandy loved riding across the island on her horses, her mother loved riding in the backseat of her limousine, with her pocketbook, handkerchief and sherry. The limousine was brought over on the barge every time Nell came down from Michigan.

When Nell bought the island, larger than the size of Bermuda, Ossabaw, Sandy likes to say, was a white elephant. Nell didn't set out to live on a barrier island away from her Grosse Pointe church and garden club and active social life. She had been living on the family yacht in the Wilmington River following the fire.

But according to Sandy, Nell seemed to like the challenge of building a new house. She found a Savannah architect, Henrik Wallin, to design the Spanish colonial revival house ("although Mother and Dad kind of designed it as they went along") and two landscape designers, Ellen Biddle Shipman, who was born in Philadelphia, and Savannah's Clermont Huger Lee, to design the grounds. Following the style of the twenties, Nell ordered imported tiles from Spain, Portugal, Italy and the Netherlands. Today, bright yellow tile with deep purple grapes and bright green leaves decorate the massive front door. The 20,000-square-foot house has a sunroom, intimate balconies on many of the bedrooms, several enclosed courtyards and ornate iron

*G*ood night and don't stick any beans up your nose.

The mannequin Lulubell with Frida, a four-legged visitor.

grillwork. In the kitchen there's a pantry with three large built-in cupboards and an eighty-year-old commercial-type refrigerator that covers one wall.

Included in the house was a standalone voice communications system, a kind of telephone intercom, presumably to alert the guests to dinner or cocktails or a ride to the beach. The phones, rounded, black, archaic, remain on the walls as a reminder of an earlier, more analog period. Now when we visit, we use our smart phone to send a text message to anyone else who might be in the house.

There are beam lights in the dining room, but they were only used to set the table. Dinner was always by candlelight, as many as seventy candles.

The twelve-by-fourteen-foot picture window in the two-story, cathedral ceiling living room overlooks Ossabaw Sound. When it was installed it was the largest of its kind. It's a product of the Pittsburgh Plate Glass Company, the family business. The room has exposed wooden beams and high up on the walls a collection of glass-eyed animals such as a black rhinoceros, an ibex antelope and a water buffalo, trophies of her father's African safari trip in the 1920s.

"There are two small sculptures on the table in the sun room," Sandy said. "One is a boy, the other a girl with an open book. They were by Paolo Troubetzkoy, a noted Russian sculptor who was commissioned by mother to sculpt us. I couldn't keep still. I was too fidgety. So mother gave me a cup of clay to keep me occupied."

In the living room there's a large oil painting of Nell, Sandy and her brother, Bill. It was painted in 1918 by Alphonse Jongers, a Canadian portrait painter (1872-1945) who was born in France.

Nell loved people. "When mother had luncheons she allowed only one nip per person. However, that one nip would knock you over. Andrew, the butler, would collect the almost empty Old-Fashioneds.

"I remember being sent to the beach every time mother had a luncheon as I would scream every time they discussed the Negroes. I couldn't tolerate their racist chatter."

Nell loved entertaining. She'd have dinner parties for fifteen to twenty people every night for eight months,

Sandy said. Many people would come from Michigan, including George Romney before he was elected governor. Women came from Savannah to play bridge.

Industrialist Henry Ford, the founder of the Ford Motor Company and a Detroit neighbor of the family in Grosse Pointe, was one of the first visitors in 1926. He was also enamored of the South, in his case, Richmond Hill, twenty-six miles from Savannah, back when the town was called Ways Station.

"He was a square dance enthusiast," Sandy said. "Every Saturday he would hold a square dance at one of his warehouses. When he came to Ossabaw he brought records and a Victrola in a wooden case that he'd wind up. We took up the tables and had a dance."

Just saying Henry Ford's name reminded Sandy of another one of Nell's irritations.

"As Mother would say, 'They were the upstart Fords. We are the chemical Fords,'" referring to one of Sandy's great-grandfather's companies, Wyandotte Chemicals Corporation.

"She had no yearning to be part of what she called 'the other Ford family from Michigan.' Detroit's Ford Hospital was named after my grandmother, Ella Neat Ford, who was married to Emory Ford, mother's father. Dad took charge of the hospital when he left Johns Hopkins. He brought all his doctor friends. When it had money problems, Henry Ford stepped in to help, but then he claimed the name."

And then Sandy was on to another Ossabaw visitor, Lily Pons, the opera singer. "Somebody in Savannah knew her and introduced us," Sandy said. "She was awfully nice. She had her picture taken in some old skunk collar of mother's. I have it somewhere."

Another favorite story involved tobacco magnate R.J. (Dick) Reynolds Jr. (son of R. J. Reynolds) and his wife. They were friends of Sandy's parents.

"Dick was married to Blitz at the time," Sandy said of Reynolds, who would have four wives. "They had spent the weekend with my parents. When they left they both wrote in our guest book. Dick said, 'I wish I could trade islands with Dr. Torrey,' but Blitz wrote, 'I wish I could trade husbands.'"

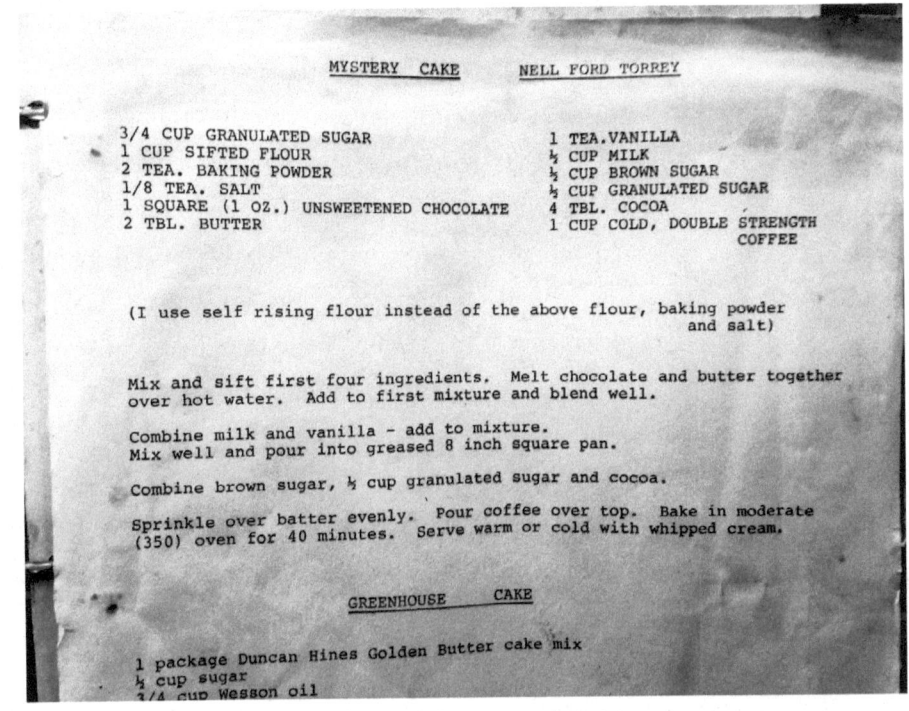

Nell's mystery cake recipe.

When Nell would come down from Grosse Pointe for the winter she would bring an entourage. The staff of eighteen included her butler, Andrew Speed; her chauffeur, Walter; a downstairs maid; an upstairs maid; waitresses, and laundresses. There was separate silverware for the help and a twenty-six-foot long Packard with spoke wheels. Nell would be served breakfast in bed with flowers on her tray. At night her butler, "with his gold fob watch, tails and a white shirt," would stand behind her chair as she ate.

"Dad didn't care much about the running of the house," Sandy said. "He hated all this stuff that went on with mother's servants. He just pretended it wasn't happening. He really wasn't much help at all. All the farm machinery was put together with Scotch tape. The superintendent was an English gardener who knew all the flowers but nothing else. Dad was busy in his head with his wonderful brain. He always had mad friends like Gar Wood, the inventor who raced boats and who owned an island in Biscayne Bay."

If her father didn't care much for domestic affairs, he was no slouch in the humor department. "I loved

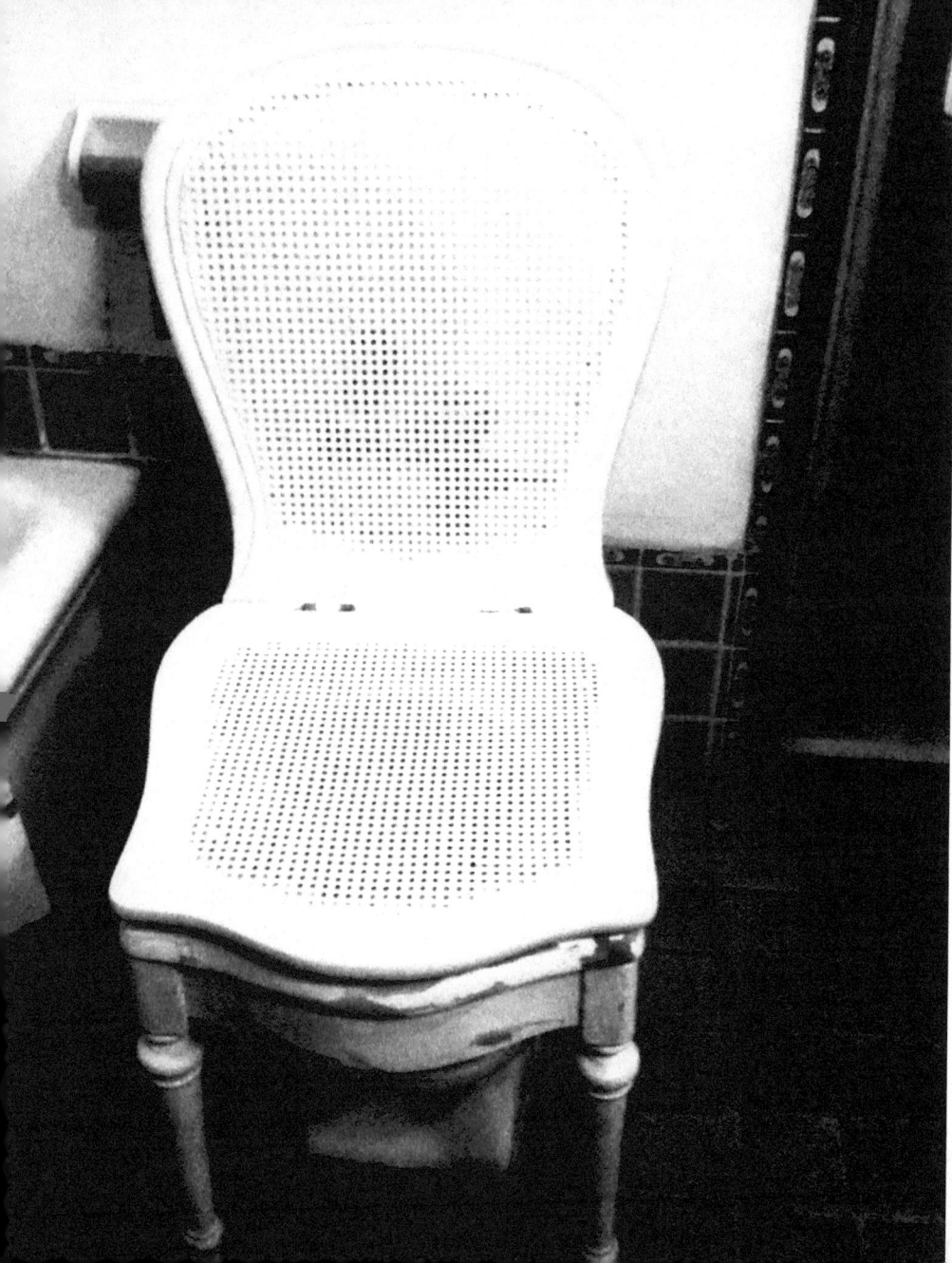

Wicker chair in bathroom.

Dad," Sandy said. "He was so funny and blessed. He had the ability to say something so funny you had to cross your legs and find a couch to lie down on. I split my sides over him. To stay awake in church he and I would count how many 'ands' and 'buts' the preacher said. Mother was very religious in a Grosse Pointe kind of way. He was so sharp."

The following note, written by Henry Torrey, greeted people who visited their yacht, the Tamarack:

Gentle hints for guests:

Please don't wear hobnails on deck.
If you insist upon this you
will have to walk on your hands.
Please don't cut the towels
with your razor.
It makes Mrs. Torrey furious.

Please don't come aboard with a good liquor appetite unless you have good liquor to accompany it. We are for Volstead — with reservations.

The Volstead Act, an act of Congress prohibiting the sale of alcoholic beverages, passed in 1919 and was repealed in 1933.

Torrey's humor extended to the house as well. Take Lulubell: She's a full-sized, fully dressed mannequin made out of beeswax. She's one of the first things you see walking into the house. She has real hair (red) and usually sits in a chair downstairs, legs crossed at a rakish angle. She's what scares people the most when they visit the house, especially if they are walking around in the dark. Henry Torrey brought her to the house from one of his trips. A recent group of furniture conservators think she came from France.

"She's almost one hundred years old," Sandy says. "Her shoes are mother's, the gown is from Ghana. I've got to fix her up. I've got her fingers in an envelope somewhere. They snapped off a number of years ago. I have a picture of her sitting on Governor Barnes' lap. Actually she's been on the lap of six governors."

During hurricane season she is brought upstairs for safety. Henry Torrey, looking for laughs, was not beyond moving her around the house.

Nell had her own brand of humor.

"Mother was a stickler about any lying," Sandy said. "If someone would call and she didn't want to talk to them she might run into the bathroom after telling me to wait a minute. She would step into the tub and say, 'Tell them I'm in the tub.' Or she might run into a room and lie down on my bed and say, 'Tell them I'm lying down.'

"Imagine that kind of person being planted in a place like this. But she loved it. She even rode horseback, though she really loved taking drives in a car. She'd look at the animals and go to the beach, all dressed up, head to toe, with her pocketbook."

"She tried ever so hard to be practical," Sandy said. "It just wasn't in her nature."

If reality wasn't her favorite thing, a turn of phrase certainly was. Sandy has adopted many of Nell's expressions. "I'm a little addlepated today," she frequently says, using a word that means confused or befuddled. "Don't worry. It doesn't have to be permanent."

Or she might say, "Good night and don't stick any beans in your ears"—another favorite of Nell's. Or, "He's as stodgy as a Stoughton bottle, dull and dumb." Other Nell expressions include, "I'm feeling a little impetudinous" (impetudinous—a variation of hebetude, dullness of mind, mentally lethargic), and "How we apples float."

Finally, if you call Sandy the first of every month don't be surprised if you hear her say, "Rabbit, rabbit." It enhances your chances of good fortune, she'll explain. Or at least minimizes bad fortune. If you forget you are allowed to say it backwards—"Tibbar Tibbar." The jury is out, she says, on whether speaking to your dog before saying Rabbit Rabbit is allowable.

All of these were favorites of Sandy but none, perhaps, so much as "epizoitical."

"Don't worry," she has said of the word. "It's not dangerous. It's not even of this world. You'll like it. I had one before Jim's (Bitler) funeral, that's why I couldn't go. Well, that's half the reason. Really, I couldn't bear it."

Sandy's brother, who came down to work on Ossabaw after quitting his job at Wyandotte Chemicals, aimed for efficiency, but Nell had her own way of looking at things.

"Once Bill came down and decided we needed a fuel furnace to save money," Sandy said. "Mother told him, 'With all this wood? Ridiculous.' Then Bill said, 'But we can get a thermostat. Then we won't need someone to be stoking the fire all the time.' Well, mother didn't say anything but she thought and thought and finally on her own she got a thermostat and installed it in the living room. Then when she would be sitting in her rocking chair and she wanted it hotter, a bell would ring and the man stoking the fire would hear and shovel in more wood. Not exactly what Bill had in mind."

There were other issues taxing her mother as the supervisor of an island home.

"One time, one of the cooks she brought down was an astrology maniac," Sandy said. "So she came to mother and said the end of the world is coming in two weeks and she would have to leave and mother would have to pay her way.

"Mother wouldn't have that. The whole place went to pieces and took sides. Mother had to stay in her room. I was the go-between. I had to bring her meals up. Dad wasn't there. It was so uncomfortable. I was impartial. I didn't dare take sides. I finally wrote a letter to Dad saying you have to come home. I gave the letter to a boat captain who was on the other side. I found out later he tore it up."

Not everyone who came down from Grosse Pointe was so enamored with Ossabaw.

"The poor maids and servants would have nothing to do on Ossabaw," Sandy said. "They hated every minute of it, those fancy Grosse Pointe servants. Once my brother Bill convinced Mother we needed cattle. She told him we couldn't keep bulls but he got them anyway. Well, one day one of the maids tried to take a walk and what did she see? A bull. Unthinkable! She came running and screaming back to the house.

"That's when mother said, 'Walter, get my car.' So Walter, dressed in a chauffeur's hat, came around. And Hamilton packed a little emporium of sherry in mother's tattered moiré silk bag along with a lace handkerchief. And off they went.

"When she saw the bull, mother calmly told Walter to stop and open the window. That's when she reached into her bag, took out a box of matches, lit this enormous firecracker and threw it out. That bull went to the south end and we never saw it again. I mean, how marvelous. Oh, she was a heavenly creature."

Chapter Six

Backed Against the Wall

When her mother died in 1959, everything in Sandy's life started to change.

"I fell heir to the island," she said. "One that everyone thought I was crazy for wanting to hold on to, including my late brother's four children," she said. Her older brother had died in 1957, her father in 1945.

"They said it was the stupidest thing I could do, that I'd lose my shirt. And they owned half, which at that time we were leasing. Well, I said I don't care. I love it. I'm going to stick to it as long as I possibly can. It turned out to be a much better investment than anyone else ever made in all their lives although it nearly killed me."

Up until that time, Sandy and her family had been going back and forth between Michigan and Ossabaw. Her brother Bill had handled most of the island's business.

But then everything shifted: the responsibility and the taxes.

At Nell's death, the island was appraised for $350,000. In 1976, the figure more than doubled to $816,612. By 1977, the county upped the number to $3,100,472.

"At the beginning, the county was glad to keep this enormous piece of land off its expense rolls," Sandy said. "Then they decided it was worth something. That's when we started to see the handwriting on the wall. That's when we started to worry. I was the only one left in the family. I knew if I didn't do something in the future my children would never be able to. I had to find a proper landlord for the island.

I don't think you can do anything well unless it's selfish.

"For eight years I explored the situation. A great many people, when they heard the island might possibly be for sale, approached me. The federal government. The state. All kinds of developers. My brother's children really loved the island but couldn't afford to keep it so they wanted to get rid of it, but I couldn't do that.

"I mean, do you know we have a live oak tree that is so big it takes eight large people to stretch their arms around it?" she said. "National Geographic wrote about it in the 1930s. They estimated it was eight-hundred-fifty-years old. That means somewhere in the eleventh century an acorn dropped and took hold. Isn't that fascinating?"

They got a bit of relief from Ted Schiwetz, an original member of the first Ossabaw Island Project board of advisors, from Texas.

"He died just when our money was really starting to run low," Sandy said. "You know that wonderful sculpture of a shark outside the house? He did that. We didn't think he had a penny. He got his sweaters at the thrift shop, but he left Ossabaw $150,000, which we used toward the taxes."

PHOTO: CARMELA ALIFFI

The money was a drop in the bucket.

The pressure was huge.

When people sensed Sandy might be vulnerable and might have to sell the island, "They started coming out of the woodwork," she said. "At the time we had a lawyer in Savannah, a blue chip lawyer. He was a real Walter Mitty. He loved the island. He always loved how many things were always going on over here, shootings and such. He lived it vicariously. One day he called and said I had to come over to Savannah right away. I said I couldn't possibly. I had just got back from Detroit. He said I had to. We were talking on one of those walkie-talkies. Then he spelled out A-C-Q-U-I-S-I-T-I-O-N, as if no one on the mobile phone could spell." Then, enjoying the memory, Sandy, who is all about a good story and can tell them well, paused to laugh.

"I said, 'I told you no. I'm not interested in selling.'

"He just kept talking," she said. "He told me, 'Well, you might be interested in this. We just received an offer from someone who wants to buy it, sight unseen, and that we should name our price, they would pay anything.' I finally said, 'OK, Julian, I'll come over and talk to you.' He said they have to know by four o'clock that day. I was so afraid someone would hear about it and make me accept it.

"Well, I went to Julian (Sipple)'s office—he was my lawyer—it turns out the interested parties who would pay anything, without even *seeing* it, were Jackie Kennedy Onassis and Aristotle Onassis," she said. "But I said I don't care. I would rather die than to have either one step on the island. That's when Julian paused a little and then said, 'Can't you just *pretend* so I could see Jackie O?' I just couldn't do it."

Later on, looking back at what she had done and at how many people had called her intractable and unyielding, Sandy would offer an expanded, more honest explanation for her decisions.

"When I started trying to save Ossabaw it was purely selfish," she admitted. "It remains so. I don't think you can do anything well unless it's selfish. If it's you who loves and cares for something then you'll fight harder than ever."

At the time she was thinking of the Georgia coast and what selling her island that "the family" had bought decades earlier might mean.

"There was a growing concern that one piece of land, one island, would contaminate the whole coast if it were developed," she said. "Sapelo was a marine institute. Wassaw was an outdoor museum belonging to the government. Ossabaw is a teaching island. It always has been. I wanted it to stay that way. To sell it would upset the whole balance of the coast. Physically, I couldn't do it. Still, I don't know anyone who turned down millions."

Meanwhile, she was growing desperate; she was conflicted.

"When I fell heir to Ossabaw—my father, mother and brother had died, my brother's children were minors—I felt absolutely overwhelmingly socially guilty to share this entire place, fifteen miles of beach and all this beauty.

"I wanted to share it, to have all these people come over. But my husband (Clifford) said, 'If you do that, you will destroy it. Let's think of another way to share it that won't destroy it.' We had been doing the professional research for a long time, having groups occasionally come out. That's when together we dreamed up the Ossabaw Island Project, and then, under the aegis of our Foundation, in 1961, Genesis and the public use and education component."

Just to be clear this was the Wests' foundation, not the nonprofit foundation (with the same name) that was formed in 1994.

"It was a way to share Ossabaw without destroying it. Do you know there have been thousands of live bodies on Ossabaw, yet you can't see a difference except for the house that mother built? We're careful not to have too many vehicles or people at one time or comfort stations. We are still hearing from children who never saw a sand dollar. People in inland Georgia don't know about the coast. The series of islands has always belonged to someone else. They're very hard to get to. I felt very lucky to share it and keep it the way it's always been."

It wasn't an easy goal. She loved their projects but the future of the island—and how they could afford to continue—loomed large. Around this time she started negotiating with the state over buying the island. During a series of unidentified recorded interviews she talked about sitting in on innumerable meetings with actuaries, appraisers, politicians and state officials when they were trying to come up with a price.

"The trouble with the state is they've been taught to confront things by the book," Sandy said. "It's all so unimaginative. It was all financial to them, of course. I'd be sitting there with the map out in front of them and they'd say, 'Oh, she is just so old. She's an old and affluent lady. She probably has X number of years to live.'" And then, because she is Sandy, because she can always step away from a situation to find some humor, she added, "Which at the time I thought was a pretty good number, you know seventy or eighty."

She continued to recall the scene. "Can you imagine, discussing how much time a person has to live right in front of them? I just sat there. Finally I said, 'Well, I want my house at Buckhead. I also want my tree.' I said I

Sandy and Jimmy Carter.

Map of Ossabaw Island from 1924.

don't want the beach. They couldn't believe it. I think for the first time Joe Tanner saw someone who was interested in something other than the financial."

Buckhead is an area of Ossabaw where Sandy kept a tree house as a retreat.

Tanner was commissioner of the Department of Natural Resources. Patricia Barmeyer, now a lawyer in private practice and a member of the Ossabaw Island Board of Directors, was acting as Tanner's legal advisor.

"There were some very, very important issues for Sandy," Barmeyer said. "The donkeys, the horses, the cows and what to do with them to keep the island a heritage preserve. She maintained her dignity throughout some tough negotiations. She's so extraordinary, so bright. Her brain is like quicksilver, as quick as anyone I know."

Then there was the issue of Roger Parker, a longtime employee of the Torrey family and of Sandy.

"The state said they wanted Roger to work for them—and not me—on the island," Sandy said. "He was the co-superintendent of the island at the time. He ran our cattle for years, among other things. But I said no. He was too good on the island. I think I'd die without him. My children weren't there. They had moved away. I had no friends who could keep up with me. Everyone loves Roger. He's John Wayne with a brain.

"Then the state hinted Robert Woodruff, chairman of Coca-Cola, was interested, but they said his company couldn't do it, that he couldn't justify the money to his stockholders. Except then it turned out Woodruff himself might do it. He wanted my foundation to continue. He was a tremendous philanthropist but mainly in the city of Atlanta."

In the end, Woodruff would be the key figure in the deal.

"Somewhere along the line I heard Woodruff's good friend, Boisfeuillet Jones, had talked to him," Sandy said. Jones was a professor, then dean at Emory University in Atlanta. From 1964 to 1988 he was president of the Woodruff Foundation.

"But none of this happened before Boisfeuillet's daughter, Laura [now Laura Jones Hardman], talked to him," Sandy said. "Laura, bless her heart, had come to the Project when she was at Emory. She got what the island is all about, how important it was to stay as it is. She told her dad he had to help save the island, which meant he had to talk to Woodruff. In the end I think it came down to Laura."

In the end, the state agreed to buy the island for eight million dollars through a bargain sale to a charitable organization, in this case The Nature Conservancy, even though people kept telling Sandy she could get much more from developers. Some said as much as sixteen million. But even that eight million was hard to come by. Eventually in a deal brokered by President Jimmy Carter, the state would come up with four million (from the taxpayers). The remaining four million would come from Woodruff himself, not his company. Woodruff, who may have flown over the island once or twice, never did visit.

In May 1978, when Sandy was sixty-five, the state took ownership. Governor George Busby signed an executive order designating Ossabaw Island the first piece of land under the Georgia Heritage Trust. There would be limited public access, no cemented airfield, no public ferry and no paved roads. Instead of overdeveloped coastal developments, such as those in Virginia, New Jersey and Florida, Ossabaw would be maintained as a "wilderness preserve, to be used solely for natural, scientific and cultural study, research and education and environmentally sound preservation of the island's ecosystem."

Sandy would have lifetime estate privileges in her house and the twenty acres around it.

In 1996, the U.S. Department of the Interior added Ossabaw to the National Register of Historic Places.

"It was a true miracle that saved the place," Sandy said. "It did not happen through the usual do-good channels where, I should say, there was absolute apathy. Some big punkin from a foundation I had gone to, a name that shall remain nameless, asked me, 'What would be second best?' I said I have never heard the word, 'second best.' Mrs. Edsel Ford said to go to the Ford Foundation but if I do I should not mention her name. And the preservation organizations, well, they paid no attention to me. It was just outrageous."

Sandy, exhausted but victorious at the negotiating procedures, received solace and support from many disparate quarters. "When everyone was fighting, threatening to throw me off the island, saying I was just keeping it for myself, I got a letter from an oyster fisherman in Thunderbolt saying if it weren't for Ossabaw Island we'd be in a terrible mess. He said, 'You have kept that vast land intact, saved our livelihood. If anyone tries to push you out I will organize all the oystermen and march to your defense.' The students said that too. They said they would march on Atlanta. That made me want to weep."

So did a letter from someone who visited the island as part of an attempt to invite "culturally deprived" children. "It said, 'Dear Mrs. West,'" Sandy said. "'I love you more than anyone in the world because you know how to leave things alone.'"

Finally, there was a postcard. It came from a member of the Carnegie family, who fought so hard to maintain the spirit and wild nature of Cumberland Island despite many disputes among Carnegie descendents about what to do with the island. Cumberland is part of a national seashore managed by the National Park Association.

"It came from Miss Lucy Ferguson," Sandy said, always careful to use "Miss" when talking about her. Lucy Carnegie Ferguson is a descendent of Thomas Carnegie, who with his wife Lucy—another Lucy in a family of many women named Lucy—bought most of the island in the late 1880s. Thomas was Andrew Carnegie's younger brother.

"Miss Lucy Ferguson is wonderful. I would like to be like her. She wrote me a postcard once—I have it somewhere—and said she heard I was having some trouble on Ossabaw, that she was having the same trouble keeping and affording her island. She wrote—I'll never forget it—'Just remember, horsey, keep your tail up.'"

Chapter Seven

Youthful Adventures

While Sandy's mother entertained in the Main House on Ossabaw and her father went off on safaris, she and her brother Bill were tutored in the upstairs rooms until they went away to school, Sandy to finishing school at Dobbs Ferry, New York, Bill to The Hotchkiss School, in Connecticut, then Princeton, in New Jersey.

But more often than not after breakfast they would go up one stairway to meet with their teachers and down another to explore the island. Between rumrunners, poachers and serpents, the island became a land of make believe. "Mother didn't know what we got into," she said.

From a 1983 interview, Sandy tells this story:

"It was during World War II and one of my good cousins from Detroit was visiting," she starts. "Someone had taken us to a beach house we had on the Atlantic side and left us there for the day. It was twelve miles away. We had that kind of freedom. We were swimming and we wore bathing caps the way people did back then. Well, when we went underwater we would hear a churning noise, like someone stepping on a starter of a car that wouldn't start. It happened from four-thirty until five in the afternoon. The next day we went swimming again and we heard the same thing. We thought it might be a shrimp boat, but when we got back we told Dad and he called the FBI. They said tell those kids to go back for three days and let us know what they hear. The same thing happened. But that was it. No one did anything and we forgot about it.

Your
hairline has rhythm.

Bill and Sandy as children.

"A long time later Joey, my cousin, was dancing with someone at the Cloisters and she mentioned what had happened to us as kids. Turns out this man was in the Coast Guard during the war and he said most definitely it was a German submarine. Can you believe it?

"And then—I've never told this to anyone before—I had my father's old German binoculars and I decided to put them on the beach for someone from the Coast Guard to find. That really caused a big fuss. Isn't that dreadful?"

In that same interview, Sandy said, "That same cousin and I rode horseback by ourselves. Fourteen miles. We saw rumrunners in a house. We saw the boat come. By that time we knew we were in trouble, that we had to stay behind some trees with the horses hoping they wouldn't sneeze until the men left the house. They were carrying great cases of stuff."

There was glamour. Like the time she danced with Johnny Mercer.

"It was after cotillion time. I was in Savannah having a marvelous time at a dance when he asked me to dance. We are about the same age. It was a brief happening but magical brief happenings are never clouded or lost. It was in the mid-thirties. I have never forgotten it and never, ever will. It happened in the crowded ballroom of the dear old Desoto Hotel. The ballroom sparkled with lights and excitement. The music made my heart thump. I was dancing with someone forgettable when Johnny Mercer cut in. I had never met him, but he was already famous so, of course, I recognized him. Can you imagine? Could anyone? We danced. We danced. Then, just as the music slowed, Johnny looked down at me and said 'Your hairline has rhythm.' I was composed on the outside and melted on the inside."

Sandy married John Shallcross in 1935. For part of that time they lived with their three children—a daughter and two sons—in Bloomfield Hills, Michigan.

"Those were the days the doctor would call on the children in the winter on horseback and then would stay for donuts and coffee," she once said. "Isn't that glorious?"

Those were also the days, she said later, that being married with kids limited her time on Ossabaw. That doesn't mean she didn't have time to travel. Much of this comes through in the book she wrote with Elizabeth Shallcross Pool, her sister-in-law, and published in 2005. While she didn't go to college Sandy's early journals are filled with poems she would write for special occasions like her mother's birthday or her aunts and quotes from Hamlet ("To thine own self be true"), Thomas Mann, Goethe, Virginia Woolfe's *Mrs. Dalloway*, Proust, Walt Whitman, Herbert Spenser, Rebecca West, Arnold Toynbee and John Ruskin.

As was her style, she had no trouble finding herself in unusual circumstances. Like the time she was traveling in New York, staying with her cousin Josephine.

"I guess I was with my John, my husband of the time, on the top floor of the Waldorf Astoria when we got on the elevator and who should get on but Salvador Dali. I mean he looked just like his picture and then this woman got on, all fancy, some big punkin, who said, 'Oh, Mr. Dali, you must come to tea.' He didn't say anything and it was terribly uncomfortable. So then I said, 'He doesn't speak English.' That quieted her down. When we got off the elevator he said to me, 'You're right. I don't speak a word of English.'"

For years Sandy had been talking to me and to others about the book she was writing with Betty Pool.

I'd ask about the book but I never got an answer I could understand, particularly—make that especially—when I'd hear the title: *The God of the Hinge: Sojourns in Cloud Cuckoo Land*.

Still curious, I'd try another line of questioning, but it's hard to tie Sandy West down. Then in her early 90s, Sandy didn't have to say anything, answer to anyone or make the least bit of sense if she didn't want to.

So I gave up. It's probably some nature book, I thought. Something about pigs or dogs or horses, all pals and/or best friends of Sandy's from her decades on Ossabaw Island. Something about the politics of giving away or selling an island to a governmental body. Or the stipulations attached to the deal. Or the way she rounded up eight million dollars. Or how she parlayed a piece of land assessed at sixteen million dollars to eight million.

Maybe, I thought, it was a book about all the brilliant people who have spent time there because the woman is generous and curious to a fault, always encouraging, inviting, inspiring people to experience (for a time) life without electricity, telephones, garbage trucks, utility bills, locks, even doors. She has something great—not fancy, but great—and she wants to share it with people who use their minds, their hands, and their imaginations.

Yes. That's it, I thought. It's a book about famous people and what can happen if they get away from the familiar.

Except Sandy isn't like that. She's not a name-dropper. She's not easily impressed. And for all the wealth she's known, she's doesn't seem to give a "rat's ass" (her words) for people with money, unless they have something interesting to say. Otherwise she'd just as soon find a shady spot near her house on Ossabaw Sound and using the backside of her pig Mrs. Musgrove as a pillow enjoy a good read and maybe a vodka martini.

If anything, I thought, once I got the book in my hands, I'd probably find it to be a nostalgic memoir about a century past when good and evil were a little more easily defined and when people acted a little more civilly toward one another (regardless of how they felt). It would tell of safaris, cruises, family jaunts, shooting parties, beach picnics, not unlike the times spent on Ossabaw.

Wrong. As Betty, who died in 2012 at age 98, writes in one of her chapters, she and Sandy are "perpetually, goose-fleshingly alert to the possible presence of Something Other. We are both astounded by life and can always be stopped in (our) tracks as we trudge the daily round." Sandy, she writes, "is a female Francis of Assisi."

This book is about friendship, curiosity and expansiveness. It's about two women with active minds, busy imaginations and sensitive antennae that extend in every direction. It's about two friends who never stop wondering or wandering, who never stop marveling or shaking their heads, who never stop piecing together clues about their time on the planet.

"Sandy's wit is inexplicable," Betty writes. "She just turns some kind of shimmering beam upon people and events and—lo! The terrain changes so unexpectedly, onlookers dissolve. Sandy's wit springs, I think, from a deep well of light. At the center of Sandy it is always dawn."

She and Betty were a pair. They were curious but they didn't want their curiosity studied to death.

Betty, sometimes called Rusty, explains it this way. "'If,' said George Bernard Shaw, 'you find something inexplicable, kindly do not attempt to explain it to me.'"

Reading between the lines, we surmise these are two upper-class women with rich husbands, perfect children, multiple homes, multiple staffs of workers and certain societal responsibilities. But there is none of that here because it's not the ironed slacks, fine hats, leather gloves and matching pocketbooks that define these women.

Early in the book, in which the two women write alternating chapters, Sandy sets the scene. "The 1930s. I arrived in New York. Steam burst from

Sandy on the beach.

Portrait of Bill, Nell, and Sandy.

the train and blinded me as I stepped down to the platform. I opened my eyes and there she stood.

"She was about my age and tall, with the darkish red hair that seems to catch minute changes of color and light. I had been told that she was scholarly and expected to be rendered speechless, but Rusty's brilliance is not intimidating. It is star-brilliant and magnetic. It enthralled and tempted me immediately and, after more than sixty years, still does—only much more so. At that very first meeting we knew one another; we were at ease, with a strange undercurrent of excitement.

"I had met her brother (John Shallcross) at a wedding in Michigan and found in him everything I wanted and nothing I could resist: marvelous good looks, rare intelligence and sensitivity, astonishing wit and the promise of adventure.

"A few months after meeting him, we met in Washington and he proposed to me upon a compost pile at Mount Vernon. I accepted with my whole heart.

"So there I was on that train platform in New York, faced with my sister-in-law-to-be. She would proceed to shake up my life."

What gets their attention is what goes on between their ears, what raises the hair on the back of their necks, what causes their stomachs to flutter. That's what they're about.

The motif for the book is travel, for which they had the resources, the time, the inclination and the desire. At a suggestion from either woman they might end up in Jamaica, Montreal, Nova Scotia, Santa Fe, Key West or Bermuda.

But this is no travel book. It's not where they go that's interesting but what happens to them when they get there. And finally—and this is what makes them so extraordinary—what they do with what they see, how they pursue what they call "symbols" and where, intellectually, their paper chase takes them.

In their search for serendipity or meaning, be it rainbows, circles, unicorns, sneezing, bells, labyrinths, harlequins or coral, they are relentless. Wherever they are, they will immediately retire to the closest library or duck into the nearest bookstore to research the symbolic meaning of whatever they perceive is dogging them.

Theirs is a life of mischief, tricksters, belly laughs, discovery and enlightenment. Along the way they become intimate with characters in mythology (especially Hermes), the field of alchemy, the extent of androgyny. Science and rationality, they would both agree—especially physics and chemistry—is the enemy.

"Hermes is like a hinged door that is never closed," Sandy likes to say. "He presides over the things people wonder about."

Without saying it, how they lived is exactly what Shakespeare's Hamlet had in mind when he said, "There are more things in heaven and Earth, Horatio,/Than are dreamt of in your philosophy."

Then there is the title. *Cloud Cuckoo Land* comes from Aristophanes' play, *The Birds*. It refers to the

Sandy and Wini Wood talk in the kitchen.

idealistic state between heaven and earth, a place Sandy and Betty often found themselves, in their travels and in their minds.

Toward the end of the book Sandy writes of another explanation:

I am beginning to suspect that this wondrous, joyous, glorious revelation is going to prove endless—a forever kind of thing. Every time we decide to write The End, we have to erase it.

Something very strange has now happened and obviously, as always, has to be contemplated. Jim (Bitler), a young friend who has been reading our manuscript, just called.

"Around ten o'clock last night," he said, "I turned the last page and was headed to bed. Instead, however, I found that I had to go out, get in my truck and drive through the woods. As if under orders, I suddenly stopped, dismounted and walked along the riverbank, arriving at a large, ancient oak, leaning way out over the water. On the trunk lay an iron shape. I picked it up and, in the moonlight, saw that it was a hinge. I also saw that it was both rusty and sandy."

With that in mind, the name, *The God of the Hinge, Sojourns in Cloud Cuckoo Land* makes perfect sense. "I've been trying these past parts of my life to go beyond words," she once said. "I'm interested in the intangible."

Chapter Eight

Queenie and Sandy

While Sandy was equipped to talk to people of all classes, she had a special penchant for longtime inhabitants of Ossabaw, many of whom continued to work for her after the state took over the island. They were all her "blessed people." They were all dear to her. They were close to the earth. And that's why she liked hanging out with them. "That's where the action is," she said.

There was Agnes Graves, who worked for Sandy for twenty-nine years, Queenie Mae Williams (the state named its Ossabaw boat for her), Sarah Parker, Mary Parker and Mable Daniels.

"They were all so enchanting and knowledgeable," she said. "Did I ever tell you about the time we sweated eggs? This is something Queenie taught me.

"You each take an egg, put it in front of a fire and sit there at eleven o'clock at night. You can't laugh or anything. You watch those eggs. At the stroke of midnight the egg of the person whose going to die first will sweat blood. At the same time a door opens and someone enters carrying a coffin of pine. Isn't that marvelous? I got a strong dose of the local culture from Queenie."

None of them escaped Sandy's irreverence, either.

"When the Project started, the first really important person coming was Roman Jakobson. He's a professor of Slavic languages from Harvard, MIT and a visiting professor from the College de France in Paris. I'll tell you,

As Queenie always assured me, "Whatever blows your frock up" or "Whatever razzes your berry."

Queenie Mae Williams.

we were a little nervous. So I told Agnes to please not talk tacky and for god sakes pronounce his name correctly. The next morning I was walking down the hall and I heard Agnes say 'Mr. Jacobs, if you crack me some pee-cans I will tickle your tootsies!' Oh, Gawd."

Alligator hunting was reserved for Sundays. People would use a fifteen-to-eighteen-foot-long pole to reach down in the alligator hole. When they caught them they would eat some and then sell the hide or meat. The gator skins hung in the "ice house" or smoke house. Alligator meat was like fried grouper or tender chicken, Sandy said. She remembers "one of my blessed people" going into the icehouse and seeing one of the "stunned" gators hanging by his tail, shaking. "It scared her to death."

Also on Sundays, folks paddled in from all over the area for church and for socializing. Church collections (coins) were put in the Jeep and buried under the Big Oak. This was when the Hinder Me Not Church was on Ossabaw. It has since moved to Pin Point, a community outside Savannah settled by freed slaves after the Civil War and boyhood home to Supreme Court Justice Clarence Thomas.

Sandy likes to tell the story of Brown Lee. This was Queenie's common law husband who lived in the tabbies, homes made of lime, sand, water and crushed oyster shells. Brown Lee had one good leg and one wooden leg. He got the peg leg when he was shot stealing chickens.

"I remember the time he was driving cattle down the river on Hell Hole," Sandy said. "That's the time his peg leg caught a tree and was pulled off. He was told to keep driving the cows so he did. Later someone came up from the rear and picked up the peg and hung it on a tree. After the drive Brown Lee went back to find his leg. When he found it high up on a branch, he said, 'I knew I was flying but I didn't think I was flying that high.'"

In *God of the Hinge*, Sandy writes, "I dearly loved a magnificent woman here on my island, Queenie Mae Williams. I knew her for seventy years. When I was a child she meant comfort without luxury, security because of confidence, joy because of happiness. As I grew older we had adventures and long talks about things that most people know nothing about.

"She was different and real with old, unchanging ways and an old, nondestructive approach to life. I suppose there was a memory of her long ago, far away African life. She had a blissful common-law husband with one leg whom she treasured and badgered. Every other weekend, with her blessing, he went to Savannah to 'hump the sisters.' I adored him.

"Then later (Oh Joy, Oh Rapture!), she shared with me a bawdy heart and a lusty soul. She sang spirituals on this island that would make your heart sing and your knees buckle. She had been a blues singer in Savannah and for years had brewed her own brand of corn likker."

This is how Elizabeth Grey Vining viewed Queenie: "At breakfast this morning Queenie, the cook, honored the group by coming into the dining room and singing, 'Lord, take my hand!' in her deep, rich voice. As she sang she walked around the table, taking each one's hand in turn. A strange and moving performance out of a lost past."

Sandy loved learning new things wherever she could find them.

"Queenie taught me things about healing, prevention of illness and trouble. Most exciting of all were our trips to town to a store that sold potions, oils, herbs, roots, and candles. Underlying everything was her faith, as firm as Mount Olympus. Today, I would give a lot to have that faith.

"I just think it's a shame no one's written down her remedies. I'd go into town with her to Tinny's Variety store. She knew the old root doctors. We went to Daufuskie, where I met this woman named Blossom Robinson. Once she told me about this blue powder she used to excite Brown Lee. 'If I put on too much he bites me,' she said. She taught me about five fingers grass. You put it at the head of the bed to save you from an evil. And there's green Spanish moss for high blood pressure. You put it in both shoes, wear them for seven days. She also sprays it in four corners of the room.

"As Queenie always assured me, 'Whatever blows your frock up' or 'Whatever razzes your berry.'

"She gave me a prayer hand once. It was a serpent ring. So pagan. I loved it."

It's from Queenie that Sandy learned never to say thank you for an herb.

And then, because Sandy was always trying to make connections between people, to find the common humanity in everyone, she remembered a guest who came to the Ossabaw Island Project. He was from Ghana.

"He was a broadcasting person, so dear. He had to keep changing his plans to come here because every time he'd get to the airport the currency in the country had changed and he had to go home to get more money.

"Well, he finally made it and had brought me all these what-nots. When I tried to thank him he said, 'No, never say thank you for an herb.' That's *exactly* what Queenie told me. So many things are the same, don't you think?"

Chapter Nine

Genesis Project

And then there was Genesis.

Nine years after thousands of thinkers, writers, artists and intellectuals from all disciplines and all countries had gathered on Ossabaw as part of the Ossabaw Island Project, Sandy had a brainstorm. This one was a doozy.

"I thought, 'What if we set aside some part of the island in a near wilderness situation for people, mainly young people, students, to come and live as close to a self-sustained life as they can?' Think of what they could learn."

After a few minutes she said, "I had the same thoughts about the groups of at-risk kids we've had out here. There are two things that freak them out the most. Total silence and total darkness. But that's such a grand way to see how nature works, wouldn't you say?"

Their emphasis with Genesis was not on famous people but on people who had the potential to be great. To have them close to the Ossabaw Island Project, which was just down the road, only added to the experience. That way, "They could talk to the famous," she said.

Sandy West is a woman who can move quickly. The idea for Genesis came in April 1970, coincidentally the first month, the first year of Earth Day. By June of that year, thirty-five students had arrived for three months. They lived at Middle Place, an old plantation site on the Buckhead River.

We
wanted them to see what quiet meant.

Sandy broadcasting seeds during the Genesis Project.

They lived in shacks or tree houses, which they built or converted as they went along. They drew water from a well. They showered outdoors. They planted an organic garden. They did not have electricity. Eventually someone contributed a milk cow ("which turned out to be a heck of a lot more expensive than milk," Sandy said). They gardened. They cooked. They survived away from their comfort zone. The tuition was ten dollars a week.

"Of course, they didn't know beans," she said recently. "This was not play-acting. This was for real. All this backpacking and natural stuff hadn't started yet. We wanted them to get back to thinking of time with the tides, of light and dark with the moon. We wanted them to see what quiet meant."

In 1972, the program went year-round. When colleges, like Shorter University in Rome, Georgia, heard about it they started offering students credit for independent study.

David Bayne, now 60, came as a science student from Reed College in Portland, Oregon. He left as a woodworker.

"I built a bird-nesting chair in the rookery," he told me. "We called it a tower house. I got interested in timber from the house, in fixing up buildings. I had no skills but I left with a focus. Genesis was very anti-establishment. It was cows and cooking."

A few semesters later he returned from Reed, this time as a builder. Today he's a furniture conservator for the New York State Office of Parks, Recreation and Historic Preservation.

"Sandy wanted us to use local trees, water oak. I remember a guy from Philly who'd change into his Speedo and sit in the middle of the lawn and meditate. He was a great painter. The place was so inclusive. I remember Roger Parker, who worked on the island, interacting with people at Genesis. We were opposites culturally. He scared the shit out of us. The whole thing was intimidating.

"It was an environmental moment. You realized you are not alone. That's what she instilled in all of us. For me, these days, it is how the environment there is affecting the house." Later on, Bayne, who graduated from Reed in 1976, added, "No one ever asked if we completed our project proposal."

If Sandy wasn't particularly interested in famous names or "big punkins" for Genesis, she got them for the Ossabaw Island Project, which existed side-by-side with Genesis, one influencing the other. Of his stay on Ossabaw, Italian sculptor Harry Bertoia said, "I thought more clearly, I found more directions in my work than ever before in my life." In that same article Roman Jakobson of Harvard, MIT and the University of Paris, said that nowhere have his studies reached "such a high degree of concentration, intensity and clarity as on Ossabaw Island."

But big names didn't impress Sandy. She is as down to earth as they come, with a wicked sense of humor to boot. She loves a good story, like the one she told about seeing academic types living in nature.

"The project was over for the season," she said. "The fellows had just left and Justin and I were in the dining room eating. We heard the back door slam. In waddled my raccoon. He climbed up on a chair, walked across the table to our centerpiece, carefully picked each piece of fruit out of the bowl. He then climbed into the bowl, went to the bathroom, and then walked back across the table, down the chair and out the back door. Slam!

"Justin and I laughed and laughed and said, imagine if that had happened while the fellows were having dinner!"

Historian H.W. Janson, professor of fine arts and chairman in New York University once wrote, "I look upon Ossabaw Island as a unique and uniquely valuable resource. The Ossabaw Island Project makes it possible for artists, scholars and scientists to pursue their work, to exchange ideas, and to refresh their spirits under ideal conditions. Genesis does the same for young people, in intimate contact with one of the few unspoiled environments along the Eastern seaboard, affording them an invaluable opportunity under expert professional guidance, to come to grips with the concept of ecology."

Although painter Alan Campbell was a member of the Project, he said something that many people from Genesis felt.

"I was at the Ossabaw Island Project," he told me. "I was just a Southern boy. I gave my presentation, about black men pouring molten lead and tobacco auctioneers. Sandy was in the audience. She said, 'It's just like a visual Faulkner.' She told me something I never forgot: 'Why do you need to go to New York and try to become who you aren't? Why don't you stay here and be who you are?'"

The first time photographer Nancy Marshall met Sandy she was intimidated—and fascinated. At the time people at Genesis were very separate from the Ossabaw Island Project.

"Sandy set it up that way," she said. "It was deliberate. But we were asked to come to the Main House to hear them give readings. When I was there, Annie Dillard was reading something from 'Pilgrim at Tinker Creek.'

"Sandy invited us to sit on the patio and have a glass of wine. My first time seeing Sandy up close, I remember thinking she could do anything. She was so open-minded. I didn't get her humor right away. She told us a pig was breaking into the house and making a nest out of some expensive coverlet. She excused herself to go upstairs and take her mother's coverlet off the bed. Now I can appreciate it."

Moose crossing.

Sandy was the force behind Genesis, said Marshall.

"It was a real gift to be able to go there. I lived in a tabby house and could see Buckhead Creek. It was more mowed down then. Cows grazed. It looked like a village. We shared labor, cooked every day, milked cows, made bread, then made the evening meal.

"I thought the place was paradise. There was no television, no telephone, no electricity. You were cast in time at this beautiful place, then more than now because you could see the water. It was very freeing. You got a lot done. I wasn't so interested in poetry but rather in seeing people who were excited by their work.

"When I was at Genesis I knew Mrs. West was the owner of the island but I was communicating with Jane Timmerman. I said, 'Who is this, Ms. West?' She was very proud of showing off her experiment. She drove and watched us. But she stayed in her cabin at Buckhead. She liked to be alone. She'd say, 'I keep it for myself. It's one thing I have for myself.'"

Helen Hamada, 63, and a former director of Genesis and now a money manager, is still good friends with Sandy.

"When I graduated from the State College of Pennsylvania, which was in a beautiful area, I didn't know what to do," she said. "I was a photography major and driving a bus for high school kids. One night when I had brought a group to a performance of prison inmates I was talking to the other bus driver who had heard of Genesis and Ossabaw so I applied and got in.

"I got there February 11, 1974," said Hamada who lives near Woodstock, New York, remembering the exact date, "and was supposed to stay two weeks. I left in July then returned two years later as the co-director. I stayed until 1980.

"I like to say I was born on that island. It was magical. There were no mirrors, no distractions. We created our own entertainment. At first we didn't see Sandy much. She'd drive around in her Toyota Jeeps she called Smiley. We were kind of known as the 'feral people,' but one day when we were on the beach and my dog got gored by a pig Sandy insisted on setting up a basket near her bed for my dog and that I sleep there in the same room. After that I'd see her typing away on her IBM, writing correspondence, trying to figure out how to save the island. She was always hoping the island would help people fix the world. I don't know about that but I did see how it changed people."

After her initial stay Wini Wood, another former project director who continues to visit Sandy, returned every January for three years. She had finished her masters at the University of Iowa and was two years into her doctorate at the University of Massachusetts. When she couldn't decide whether or not her doctorate would be in syntax (or semantics) or phrenology, she returned to Ossabaw, where she washed clothes by hand, wringing them out with a manual wringer, and helped build an A frame house. She stayed two years, "until Sandy ran out of money and I had to leave."

Now she teaches language and film at Wellesley College.

"Ossabaw was the most important place I'd ever been," Wood, 63, said. "It was a bridge. Because of the physicality of being on an island I could forget my body. It never felt bad to be alone at Genesis. It felt safe, secure and secluded in the middle of the island. It changed the lives and livelihoods of a lot of people."

Some of Wood's experiences were memorialized in Ross McElwee's quirky and prize-winning 1986 film, "Sherman's March: An Improbable Search for Love." When McElwee asked Wood what a linguist such as herself hoped to achieve on Ossabaw, she answered, "Time to be alone and to think. Time to get away from theoretical feuds."

In the film, she said she used to think there were only two important things in life—linguistics and sex. "I now think there are other important things," she said, while milking a cow. When pressed she grinned and answered, "I am very fond of this cow."

During one visit when Helen Hamada, Sandy and I were sitting around, looking at the painted buntings visiting her bird feeder, petting her dog, Toby Two, and shooting the breeze, Sandy said, "Wouldn't it be wonderful if the island broke loose and we wouldn't know where we landed? It would be like never-never land."

No less a luminary than David Brower, founder of the Sierra Club and Friends of the Earth, wrote, "Ossabaw Island teaches me every time I am fortunate enough to set foot here. There is much more to be learned—so much more by so many others—that its natural university, the essential part of a coastal exhibit essential to the whole earth, must surely be left to find its own way to teach those who are to arrive perceptive, or who will be sensitized here. There are no other Ossabaws where this one came from. It holds answers to questions man has not yet learned how to ask."

Larry Earl, an early Genesis participant, put it another way. "Living in nature is different than loving nature," he said. Peter Schellhorn, another Genesis member, said, "We were part of an ecological movement, especially since there were plans to link the causeway on Ossabaw with Jacksonville (Florida). I saw them. Just think about that for a minute. It could have happened, you know."

Chapter Ten

The Multiplier Effect

Many of the people who came over for Genesis or for the Project stayed in touch with Sandy. Either they fell in love with the island or the person or both. Photographer Nancy Marshall is one of these people with a double love.

The last time Marshall spent time with Sandy, the South Carolina resident shared news of her daughter, Kate. "I told her she's an environmental lawyer," Marshall related to me during a visit to her home in McClellanville, where she lives on the edge of the marsh—and the continent—with her husband, photographer and printmaker John McWilliams. "Without missing a beat Sandy said to me, 'See? The influence keeps going.' That's who Sandy is."

And so it goes because that is exactly what ecologist, teacher and long-time Sandy pal, environmentalist John "Crawfish" Crawford, says about Sandy.

"What's she's done has had a multiplier effect," he said. "She'd say what was important to her was to diligently and successfully make the place available to a huge spectrum of people and that's exactly what's happened."

Marshall met Sandy in 1978 when she visited Ossabaw as part of the Genesis Project. She had seen photographs of the eerie and stark boneyard beach and thought, "Oh my god, how do I get there?" She applied for and received a residency. That was the beginning of a long friendship, one of many Sandy can claim.

She's excited about stuff she already knows but wants to know more about.

Artists on a trip to Ossabaw. Melody Postma, Susan Dennis, Julio Garcia, and Marcus Kenney.

It's those friendships that are key to Sandy's longevity, said Crawford of the woman who turned one hundred and one in 2014. "She's fun to be around. She has a great sense of humor, good self-worth, and she is cherished by people who know her. She's excited about stuff she already knows but wants to know more about. I do believe that's a key to her longevity.

"My mother and uncle grew up here on Isle of Hope," Crawford said of a Savannah neighborhood on the water. "My uncle, who knew Sandy, likes to say, 'She was the most beautiful woman I've ever known.' When I met her she was very much the same as she is now. Of course, people age. We change. But this is the person I've always known."

McWilliams, who met Sandy later through his wife, Nancy, echoes Crawford's assessment.

"She's just so interested in everything,"

Carmela Aliffi and Kelli Rose Pearson.

he said. "About two weeks ago Nancy and I were visiting and saw about fifty vultures flocking around the fountain. When I told Sandy she said straight away, 'Vultures are a sign of longevity.' Then she told us about a nesting place at Middle Place and that she wanted to go there, so we got in the car and took her. She had her digital camera and went right up to the nest to take pictures.

"It's the most amazing thing. Over the last few years so many animals have died off, but what's still incredible is to sit on the front stoop of her house and see these animals start to appear. The few remaining donkeys, the vultures, the horse, the pigs. The vultures stuck around, in the patio. We stayed in the blue room, watching them. They're very intelligent. They trade objects. They'd sit on the wall and converse. Sandy said it'd been a dry summer and they were looking for water."

There is a fulltime pig-killer on the island to keep the population down.

"But it was always something. Animals would circulate around the house. We'd see the goose talking to the horse. They went on and on talking, reacting, making noises. It's a wild place. Every time I go I am deeply affected by what goes on around it. The pigs alone are a reflection of that.

"We go about twice a year but when we show up we just take up where we left off last time. I'm amazed at her ability to recall conversations I had with her ten years ago."

That reminded me of something Sandy said to her friend, Gordon Varnedoe. This was during a gathering on Ossabaw to celebrate Sandy's one-hundredth birthday. People were there from all over. It was chaotic. Everyone wanted to talk to her. When it was Gordon's turn, he leaned over and kissed her and said he missed her. Then Sandy, without hesitation, asked about Gordon's daughter, Nell, who had been ill (and who died in 2014) and Gordon's wife, Catherine, who couldn't come. That didn't surprise me as much as what followed.

"How's Sweet Pea?" Sandy asked, somehow remembering the name of Catherine's horse.

During the 2013 Ossabaw Island Pig Roast, Picnic, and Art Sale, the only fund raising event hosted by the Ossabaw Island Foundation, I watched Sandy carry on numerous conversations, many at the same time. Known simply at "the pig roast," it is held on Sandy's expansive front yard. It is casual and sometimes a little taxing on Sandy.

But when approached by Patricia Barmeyer, a board member of the Ossabaw Island Foundation, who said, "Sandy, your note to my father was darling. You're the only one-hundred-year-old to send a greeting that said, 'Welcome to the club,'" Sandy didn't flinch.

"It's true," Sandy said. "How many of us *are* there?"

Later Barmeyer told me Sandy had emailed her father and said one of the best things about being that age is knowing the pleasure her children get from telling people their mother (or father) is one hundred.

During a recent visit after the Pig Roast, Sandy started talking to Nancy and John about a car her niece, Torrey, gave her. She was very proud of it, McWilliams said. But she wanted to brand it as her own.

"She said, 'I want to make it mine.' So I said, 'Well, I'll paint a pig on it if you want.'"

For the past five Pig Roasts, McWilliams has created a woodcarving of the signature Ossabaw pig for the front of the invitation.

But there's no predicting Sandy. About the car, she had another idea.

"That's when she said, 'I want Toby on it. Can you do that? Can you do it today?'"

"So I did, right then and there," said McWilliams. "She was involved in every phase. Trey (Coursey) went looking for some rustoleum. I did a preliminary sketch. And then Sandy pulled her chair up close to the car to watch. That's the quality she has—nothing is impossible. It's beautifully childlike."

Now the car with Toby's picture on the driver's side door is among the first things she points out to visitors.

At another visit Nancy showed Sandy some black and white photographs she had taken on an earlier trip.

"She got right into the picture," Nancy said. "She said the moss on the tree was like a curtain you have to see through. She was saying, 'Should this be lighter or darker?'

"When I showed her pictures I took of Poco, her old horse who must have been around thirty when she died, Sandy she said she looked like a beautiful old lady. Then she said, 'I can see wrinkles and bones and she's still beautiful.'"

This was the visit Marshall and McWilliams got to see Sandy painting with artist Betsy Cain.

"She wanted me to see the paintings," Marshall said. "It was the neatest thing to watch them together. There was Sandy painting on her breakfast tray and Betsy getting her scissors out, finding brushes, getting her water. Then Betsy got in bed next to her and said, 'You go first.' She did a line and then Betsy did one, kind of like the exquisite corpse way or producing a painting. Sandy was very focused. An hour later they were still working on the same painting."

Chapter Eleven

Justin and the Bunny Rabbit

One week before Sandy West's one-hundredth birthday, the Ossabaw Island Foundation invited friends to a celebration at the Coastal Georgia Center in Savannah as part of the Foundation's annual meeting. Sandy intended to address the crowd via Skype, but when she said she wasn't feeling up to the event, her son, Justin, took her place.

Justin, 61 at the time, lives in Northampton, Massachusetts, where he is an electronic media professor at Holyoke Community College. Some of Sandy's nicknames for Justin—she claims she has fifteen—include Justoon, Tuners, Datoon, Tinian and Tinny.

As Mary Landers reported the next day in the Savannah Morning News, Justin sent along a few words from his mother. "She said the crazy thing is when you get to be old you start for the first time in your life looking backward and wanting to be young again. She's decided that's silly. What she'd like to tell you is she is not going to look back. She is going to look forward. Because she may be one hundred years old but those one hundred years have given her an insight, a curiosity and an inspiration for life she's never had before."

For those of us who know Sandy and understand her distress over the island's recent technological and/or cyber connectivity to the mainland, this was an interesting message. She, like many of us, is conflicted about instant communication. We like it—especially after we get used to it—but we like quiet, too.

*S*he said the crazy thing is when you get to be old you start for the first time in your life looking backward and wanting to be young again. She's decided that's silly.

Sandy painting in bed.

Once I was staying on the island after one of Sandy's falls when Justin and family felt it would be good to have an extra set of hands around. I camped out in the room across from hers so I could hear if she needed me. It's my favorite bedroom. It faces the Ossabaw Sound. At night I can see the moon rise over the horizon and cast a long trail of white on the water; in the morning, there's the sun, a brilliant orange. There is a five-foot bathtub in the bathroom. And, like many of the other bedrooms, there is a decorative woven and wooden lid covering the commode.

It was mid-afternoon. I had just returned from a long walk with Sandy's dog, Toby. I walked up the main stairs leading from the wooden, high-ceilinged living room and knocked on her door. She didn't answer. I eased it open, expecting to find her in a deep sleep. No one was there. This is not good, I thought. Not knowing what to do, I headed down the long hall to the other set of stairs that lead to the kitchen. On my way I saw a figure in the office. It was Sandy, hunched over the computer, peering into the screen.

I choked back my feeling of relief and asked what she was doing. "Checking my email," she said, as if it were the most natural thing in the world to do. "Look at these pictures Justin sent. They're absolutely marvelous."

A few weeks later Justin came to the island for a visit. He and I met at a coffee house on Isle of Hope. The day before, he told me, he and his mother had left Ossabaw, docked Sandy's boat at the DNR dock at Vernon View and piled into Justin's rental car. They were headed to the Apple Store in Charleston, South Carolina. They were shopping for a new computer, an iMac.

"Every time you doubt her she wiggles her way out, then you realize you were not paying attention," said Justin. "We had gone to the Apple Store," he said. "They put her on a stool at the Genius Bar and got one of those young people who work there to talk to us. I wanted to set her up with a Facetime camera so I could fix the computer for her from home.

"I thought we had had a good visit and she was all hooked up, but when I got back to Massachusetts I got a call. 'OK, Moosie,' I started, using the nickname I had given her a long time ago because I thought the waves of her hair looked like the antlers on a moose. 'What's wrong with the computer?' Turns out she was still pissed at all the kids in the store for playing with screens instead of playing outside doing something."

When I asked Justin what he admired most about his mother, he barely hesitated. "Her flexibility," he started. "She went from riches to rags and was still OK with it. Some wealthy people have a hard time with their self-esteem. Not mother. She's got an everything-is-interesting attitude. She thinks about something before deciding. That type of attitude is impossible to inculcate in my students. I might say, 'Want to watch a black-and-white movie?' They say, 'Nah. Watch black and white? What's that about?' But then they ask, 'Will it be on the test?' as if that was the bottom line.

"She grew up before TV, cell phones, computers. She had maids, chauffeurs, never balanced a checkbook let alone all the technology no one had thought of," he said.

Later on, he said, "My mother was a society woman. She had a sensibility, a latent interest in art. When the island fell heir to her, my father cowed her to do something artsy. They were among the first people to come up with an interdisciplinary system."

At that point Justin excused himself to take a call. It was from his wife, Eileen, who was still on Ossabaw.

"The bad news is Paul, the hog, might be sick," Justin told me when he hung up. "The good news is at least it's not my mother."

When Sandy lived in Birmingham, Clifford taught at Cranbrook and Justin went to Roeper City and Country, a liberal, freethinking private school that didn't have any grades.

"George Roeper was to the school the way my mother was to the island," Justin said. "It was an alternative school. The college I went to was the same way. I didn't get my first grade until graduate school at the University of Massachusetts in Amherst. I said, 'What's this?'"

Justin went to the New College of Florida in Sarasota, Florida, then Hampshire College in Amherst. He graduated in 1977.

Justin's bunny drawn by Jane Fishman.

Because of his age, Justin has no memory of Sandy's brother, Bill, who died in 1957 (or the two houses of Sandy's childhood—Clearview and Greenwich). He doesn't remember either set of grandparents. But he does remember the Ossabaw of his youth. "We'd come down every Christmas and Easter," he said. "We took the train to New York or Washington D.C., then switch to another train. There was nothing I wanted to do more than go there. We had boats and animals. Fifteen people thought of you as family. There was machinery and electrical things to look in on. I took care of animals, built a smokehouse. My other three siblings didn't come as regularly."

When Sandy's mother died in 1959—her father died in 1945—she and her brother Bill Torrey's four children inherited the island. "We leased the Torrey half," Justin said.

Justin and his parents spent several years in Europe. While they were there they bought him a stuffed animal. They called him, "Bernard the Bunny." According to Sandy, "Justin and I use it for either an unfortunate illness or a big adventure. Whoever is sick gets him. Justin sent him to me last month for my hernia operation. It's filled with an herb called 'everlasting.' It's Justin's oldest doll. He's wearing a sash from the France, a ship we traveled on to Europe. "He needs some repair, perhaps a nose job."

Justin understood his mother's decision to sell the island to the state.

"We had to sell it," he said. "To go one more generation we would have had to pay death taxes, almost $20,000 a year. She was being taxed like she lived in Savannah. She sold it for eight million dollars even though at one time it was assessed for sixteen million and could have maybe gotten it if she had held out. (Robert) Woodruff from Coca-Cola gave the state half of that to buy it."

Stopping for a minute, Justin sighed and said, "She went through huge amounts of money."

She underwrote the cost to transport hundreds of people to the island, to support them while they stayed there and to pay a staff to feed them. She was generous.

The distressing part, Justin said, is that, "Once she's gone we can never go to the island again. She didn't keep any acreage for the family. She didn't put aside any money for herself, either, for old age."

Based on the comments in the guest book that "lives" in the kitchen, Justin's son Beryl, now in his twenties and on the board of the Ossabaw Island Foundation, loves the island as much as his grandmother.

"Oh Moose!" he writes, using the family nickname for Sandy that has stuck for so many years. "So many amazing memories are made on this island. My life would not be anything without this place. I just love it and you so much. As much as the SUN, the MOON and the foaming OCEAN TIDE. I love you. Beryl. April 17-April 24, 2005."

Another time Beryl wrote, "Stretcher please!" using a phrase special to Sandy, Justin and Beryl, referring to bouts of hilarious laughter. "Congratulations on being a published novelist at 93!"

And then, "Yesterday I was sitting in the red truck in the middle of Buckhead Field. I was sitting between two of my favorite people in the world. We were all laughing hysterically. So much so, that the truck had to be stopped. And to top it all off I was in the most beautiful and important place in the whole world. You really can't ask for more than that. I love you so much. Beryl. March 15-20, 2010."

Chapter Twelve: A Coca Cola Sign and a Pair of Boxing Gloves

Sandy has a soft spot for serendipity, for the happy accident. She believes in it. She lives it. She managed to write a whole book about it with her friend and sister-in-law, Betty Pool. *God of the Hinge, Sojourns in Cloud Cuckoo Land* is about what happens when you leave yourself open to discovery. It sounds easier than it is, even for people who believe in it, especially in this age of technology when most answers are at our fingertips.

In the mid-seventies, Sandy was facing a brick wall. In 1976, the island was assessed $816,612. The next year the figure jumped to $3,100,472. At that point, Sandy knew that neither she nor her brother's heirs could afford to pay the taxes. Anticipating this, she had spent the eight previous years looking for an angel or a solution. None was forthcoming. Then, after some intervention, she was about to close a deal with the state. She would sell them the island for eight million dollars in a bargain sale. In return she would be granted a lifetime estate and the state would agree that Ossabaw would not be developed, there would be no roads, no airstrip, no regular ferry from the mainland.

Still, she was conflicted.

She wrote about this time in her life in *God of the Hinge*.

"I hated having to do this, but there was no alternative. I would continue living on the island, but I just couldn't be in complete charge any more. The state of Georgia seemed the best landlord.

*N*ow I feel like I did before. Not to give up.

Sandy and Trey.

"A large sum of money was lacking to close the deal and at the last moment Mr. Robert Woodruff of the Coca-Cola Company donated it. Now there was no doubt about what I had to do, but I was devastated. Was I absolutely sure I was doing the right thing? I needed one more week to make a final decision.

"I went to the beach to take a quiet walk, always my solution to any problem. As I was meandering sightlessly along, I almost fell over a huge, round, heavy, metal disk laying half on the sand and half in the ocean. It was about two feet in diameter, bright red and on it was the familiar logo, COCA-COLA. There it was and there was my answer.

"I brought the sign back to the house and here to this day it hangs in the hall. It is in perfect condition—not a scratch.

"Some months later, a friend brought to visit a man high up in the Coca Cola hierarchy. My friend asked me to tell him the above saga, which I did and took him to see the sign. "That sign is seventy years old," he said in wonder. "I don't see how it is possible for it to have been where you found it. It's too heavy to float, too shallow to hold air. Why didn't it sink? And, if it did, and was washed ashore, why isn't it scratched? Now let me think—we should measure the underside to see if the amount of air could possibly…"

"Just a minute," Sandy told me she said, unable to resist. "Why do people always think there has to be a logical explanation for everything?" The man, flummoxed, left soon after.

Then there is the case of the miniature plastic boxing gloves. This serendipitous activity happened sometime after the deal with the state was struck. Still, issues had to be worked out, issues that kept her up at night.

The Coca-Cola sign.

Sandy told me this story when she was in her early nineties, before I read her book, before I knew her well enough to believe in her stories. I had been keeping her company after her hernia incident when she had to go to the hospital on the mainland in the middle of the night, a boat trip she described as "magnificent. I was so excited by the phosphorescence in the water."

She may have been bed-bound. She may have been recovering. But she could still follow the dots. Her mind was on a "thinking tour."

"See that little cloth bag hanging on my bedpost?" she said to me. "Take it down. I want to show you something."

This was a time when there were two single beds in Sandy's bedroom, one for sleeping, the other for her "desk." Later, trying to create a clear path to the bathroom and the rest of the room, well-meaning people would eliminate the second bed to create more room. It was probably a good idea but at the time I thought the second bed and the space it offered was pretty clever, especially for people—like myself—who prefer to see everything we are working on. No file cabinets for us. No computer files either.

Jaw and teeth in the side of a tabby house.

PHOTO: CARMELA ALIFFI

I retrieved the small leather bag, untied the string and took out the plastic though worn gloves. They fit easily in the palm of my hand.

"I was walking as I always do, my mind wandering," she said. She was looking for answers, for connectivity, the way she and Betty Pool used to do on the trips they would take together. She was looking for meaning. It could be a color, a shape, an object or a rainbow. It would be something involving Hermes—her favorite Greek god. The playful Hermes was known for his cunning and shrewdness and ability to carry a message.

"Hermes," she has said, " is like a hinged door that is never closed. He presides over the things people wonder about."

She paused and looked down at the boxing gloves.

"I found the first one years ago on Bradley Beach," she said. "That's where I go when I'm stricken or upset. The state had just announced my horses would have to leave Ossabaw. That upset me a great deal. We had already been fighting about what and how often people could hunt the pigs. I looked down in front of me and there it was, one boxing glove, sand-colored and stuck in the beach.

"I knew right away what it meant. It was a sign to keep fighting. Otherwise it didn't make any sense. I mean, why else would I find this?"

The irritations continued. Even after settling with the state about what should happen to the island, there were new issues. Sandy was facing other challenges—her horses the states wanted moved, the number of days set aside for hunting, maintenance of

The boxing gloves drawn by Jane Fishman.

roads—the day Trey Coursey came to visit. For the past few years Trey has assumed main caretaking responsibilities at the house. Before that he lived on Ossabaw as part of the Ossabaw Island Foundation.

"Two days ago that dear Trey came and said he had found something on the beach past the tabbies. No one goes there," Sandy said. "It's my special place. 'You won't believe this,' Trey said. Then he opened his hands and gave me the match to my boxing glove. The exact same thing.

"Think what this means," she said. "Isn't it unbelievable? Did you ever? All this fighting? Right when I'm falling backwards and money is scarce and there's one crisis after another, I find this. Now I feel like I did before. Not to give up."

Chapter Thirteen

Sandy and Jim

Sandy West has had many wonderful people in her life. She attracts them. She gathers them around her. She encourages and challenges them. Jim Bitler was one of these people. Sandy and Jim shared a robust sense of humor, an intense love of nature and an impatience for anything phony. For the seven years Jim lived on Ossabaw as the on-island representative of the Ossabaw Island Foundation, he drank coffee with Sandy, shared a nip or two in the afternoon and exchanged stories. After Jim's untimely death in 2011 we found several notebooks where he had transcribed some of these conversations. Jim often talked about putting together a book of Sandy's bon mots. In the spirit of this intention I offer these notes.

But first a newspaper obituary I wrote that sad day in April when Jim died too young, too soon.

Jim Bitler, the face of Ossabaw Island, the on-island working stiff of the Ossabaw Island Foundation, the go-to man for Sandy West, who gifted the island to the state of Georgia thirty years ago, died Sunday afternoon while taking a nap. He was fifty-five. Paul Pressly, the Foundation's Education Alliance Director, was on the island at the time. Pressly knew something was amiss after he called Bitler repeatedly, only to get Jim's upbeat and unmistakable message: "If I don't answer, chances are I am somewhere on this beautiful island loving my job."

If I don't answer chances are I am somewhere on this beautiful island loving my job.

Jim Bitler preparing some mushrooms he called "chicken of the trees."

Few can boast so much love for their job. Accompanied by his two Boston terriers, Beau ("that's Beau-regardless," he would say) and Kate ("Katherine the Great"), Bitler would greet visitors at the dock, load them in his truck, drive them to their quarters and start the magic. Through him, the island's history came alive. He was scientist, raconteur and naturalist. He could point out the island's eleven long leaf pine trees. He knew the gestation period of an armadillo (one-hundred-twenty days), how to identify and cook "chicken of the tree" (an island mushroom) and just the right amount of oyster shells, lime, sand and water to recreate the original tabby surface of the three standing slave cabins on the island's north end.

His quarters were simple, his mind a steel-trap retrieval system. He was a stand-up comedian. If he bumped up a story a notch or two, it was only to make it better. To Sandy West, his longtime compatriot and co-conspirator, the impish Bitler was "Pieface" or "James James Morrison Wethery George Dupree Milne." He taught himself to make baskets out of sweet grass. He was a watercolorist. He grew indigo.

Bitler, who spent seven years at Ossabaw, graduated from Ohio State University with a degree in wilderness skills. As a naturalist he worked for Little St. Simons, Wilderness Southeast, the Sea Island Company and Disney's Hilton Head Resort, where he was employee of the year, "which meant I had to walk across the stage in giant Mickey Mouse shoes in front of Maya Angelou, who was speaking."

After Jim's death, Elizabeth DuBose, director of the Ossabaw Island Foundation, found a stack of notebooks in Jim's quarters. They were filled with delightful transactions between Sandy and Jim. Following, with Jim's partner Jack Sinopolis' permission, are a few of the notations. For the most part the selections are how Jim recorded their conversations, some entries with dates, some without. In some instances I have tried to clarify items in parenthesis.

August 27, 2003

A chance happening with Sandy. I dropped by the house at 6, well after Sandy is usually retired for the day. I went to sketch the tiles surrounding the front door. I pulled up to the house and set up and noticed the kitchen light on so I strolled down the hall and knocked at the kitchen door. "Come in."

We smiled and chatted and she offered me a glass of wine ("join me in the 'wine department'"). We spoke of strong people who took a stance… and fought to get what they want…. As a woman the fact that she had money gave her perspective and strength. "I had money and answered to no one. I had my ideas/goals and wasn't dependent on others; didn't have to negotiate. I wanted what I wanted and was in a position to underwrite my wishes without outside approval or conditions."

October 14, 2003

We talked of the "Wishing Chair." Retrieved from Greenwich. It's Chinoise obviously. There is an identical chair on Jekyll in one of the cottages. Apparently folks were permitted to sit in it and make a wish for 25 cents. Since learning this, this chair (here on Ossabaw) has been referred to as the wishing chair.

October 16, 2003

"The 'gates' at the state entrance were originally at the entrance to Greenwich, our family's winter home from 1917-1923 when it burned. After the sale of Greenwich to Bonaventure the gates were ours and we thought should be taken to Ossabaw. They were loaded and chained on a shrimp boat at Vernon View and ferried across. En route the gates shifted and slid to one side. The captain ordered the chain cut to keep the boat from capsizing. The gates slid off the deck, anchor buoys were dropped at the site and later a crew returned and retrieved the gates." They now hang at the entrance to the Torrey West estate.

November 2, 2003

"I don't eat meat generally. I read a book which described the processing of animals. I just couldn't endorse it. I have never minded eating meat from the island as I know that island animals have had a good life and a good death."

April 1, 2004

Sandy wanted to see the dogwoods along Hell Hole Road and at 5 p.m. we headed out from the house after viewing the white truck stuck in a deep hole in the backyard. Apparently she had attempted to head out on her own.

I pulled into the Middle Place field beautifully greened up. There were the four donkeys. Sandy got out and called them. They strolled directly to her. She thought one was pregnant so she got down on all 4's to peek under it to sex it.

From there it was back to the main road and a left on Long Old Field Road. We wandered through the forest stopping at a depression full of water covered with duckweed. She remembered all the frogs that would circle the perimeter and how they would plunge in leaving frog shaped outlines in the duckweed. It's too cold yet but come back and see it, she said. It's quite special.

From there we hit Half Moon Road and paused where the creek runs close to the forest on the left. "See that big bend in the creek?" she said. "That's how Half Moon got its name. I remember oyster roasts here."

The sparkleberry trees were bright green with new growth. Somewhere off to the right is a stone marker with a roman numeral on it. There are a couple we have found. We hit Willows, turned right then a left on Hell Hole. We found Celia, Poco and Phoenix (her horses) meandering through the woods. She called out, but they didn't recognize the Rover and we didn't have any food for them so they kept their distance. Lovely to see them roaming freely through the forest.

"Lots of dogwoods though a bit less than in the past," Sandy says. Eventually we hit South End Beach Road and headed home through Hut camp South End Road. Mile Marker #6 is off to the left at the causeway leading to the main house where marsh is separated from old duck pond where flotsam collects. She has a copy of the 1824 map that shows the mile markers. Will check it out. Sandy: "This map was made with imagination but not without some observation."

We heard a chuck-will-widow (a nocturnal bird), the first of the season. Sandy remembers when the whip-poor-wills would be calling around the main house. "Dad would put up with it for awhile then grab his shotgun, go outside in his pajamas and fire up into the air to quiet them down."

April 5, 2004

Phone calls. To the left as you head along Rice Pond Road is a large clearing. That used to be full of fresh water and that's where they used to grow rice. "Check out the road that runs along the fence just the other side of the gates. The tongue oil trees are in bloom as I've never seen. Mother planted a few there and they have just taken off."

April 15, 2004

Phone message:
James James Morrison Morrison
Weatherby Dupree
He said to his mother
To his mother said he
Don't go down to the edge of town

Without consulting me.
… So I'm consulting you

James James Morrison Morrison
Weatherby George Dupree
Took great care of his mother
Though he was only three
He said to his mother, his mother
To his mother he said said he
You must never go down to the end of town
Without consulting me.
(Part of an A.A. Milne poem)

May 19, 2004

Went to Sandy's room to watch a video of "Natural South." Turner Broadcasting is coming here to film June 1.

"Dobbs girls didn't wear lipstick when I was at Dobbs. Bill Torrey (her brother) paid one of his friends to come to Dobbs to visit me.

Sandy at Camp Eleanor.

"Back then we had to sit upright across from each other in the sitting room. We sat in silence. We were also allowed to 'walk the circle,' which was like going around the clubhouse.

"So there we were, walking and not saying a word. I had tucked my compact under my skirt. I feigned needing my compact and powdered my nose. Back then, compacts were powder on one side and rouge on the other. Imagine my horror when I went to my room after he left and looked in the mirror. I applied the wrong side and had a bright red nose."

"I've always been able to fight for what I believed because I had a lot of money."

"Mother was 40 when I was born and 89 when she died."

Watched footage of her marriage to John (Shallcross). 12 bridesmaids and 12 ushers/groomsmen. At one point while the bridesmaids were being panned while standing on the porch of Clairview, Sandy said, "They are probably dead as smelts." She said they were married in 1935.

There are Lenox dishes with a gold band run down the middle with EFT. They were created for the rehearsal dinner.

SOME REMAIN NAMELESS, good title (for a book)

July 12, 2005

"Mother was a perfectly respectable Presbyterian but she got it in her mind that Bill and I needed to be Baptized... we were 10 or so. She bore us downtown to a church with a Baptismal emporium. We changed into a white gown and stepped down in the pool....or bathtub? Swam across to the minister or deacon at which point I was stood up and bent over backwards, dipped my head under the water."

August 22, 2005

Sandy read Paul's *NEH* rough draft. She only found a couple mistakes. "People always leave the 'e' off "Gross." People always say Aaron Copeland was a project member. Not true. Sammy Barber, god I adored him, got Aaron interested in the Project. Aaron then became a board member, but never actually came here."

August 23, 2005

"Gardening with a Matriarch"

Dealing with Sandy is a lot like gardening. You plant the seed the night before the occasion, water the next morning (fertilize if new), then hope a storm (or drought) doesn't hit in the meantime. See definition of matriarch.

October 2, 2005

On the ceremony of death, "I hate the idea of funerals. Why make people go through the grief twice? Jill (her daughter) said, 'what about the many people who need to say goodbye? (Sort of!).' I told Jill if 'they' felt the need for a funeral I would understand. Funerals are after all for those still around. I'll be gone.

"But the essence is to those in the immediate circle (family) to do as they know is the person's wishes. After that it is for the others."

November 30, 2007

During our daily morning check-in chat Sandy was reviewing her "things to do today" list, one of which was needing to email a book to Hoagie Carmichael. I'll be interested to see what that actually means.

July, 2008

Me: "Can you still open a bottle wine or do you want me to open it for you?"

Sandy: "Oh, certainly. The only thing is when I do it I, of course, press it to my bosom at which point I end up calling life-line and need to apologize."

Chapter Fourteen

Sandy, Lisa and Louisa

Whatever else is happening in Sandy West's life these days—a pending visit from one of her four children; a morning report from Trey Coursey, her most constant on-island caretaker, the one who keeps her on track; or a painting session with Betsy Cain, another frequent caretaker—there is the mid-morning phone call.

"Hello, lovie," Sandy will say, picking up the old-fashioned landline receiver, sometimes dragging it by the cord to her ear. And not always by the first try. "This Saturday? That should work. Tell Trey."

And then she'll lapse into something about Toby, her dog, or some "tasty" man from the DNR or maybe some amazing dream. It could be something entirely unrelated.

"Oh, lovie, did I tell you? Some muckety-muck asked me to be on a committee about trees and if I did agree to do it, the prize would be four trees. Can you imagine? Where would I put them? I am so blessed to be living here."

By this time, after visiting for some eight years, after hearing the one-sided playful yet intimate and comfortable conversation, I have a pretty good idea who is on the other end of the line. I have been listening to their conversations long enough to say a silent prayer to anyone out there who might be hearing this: "So, here's the deal: If I promise to be good, if I mind my Ps and Qs, if I do enough good deeds, could you promise to be sure to send me a friend this attentive, this patient, this good-natured when I am one hundred years old, or maybe a few years earlier? Please?"

*I*t's her dogged determination to fight for what she believes is just.

Lisa White, Louisa Abbot and Sandy at Sandy's 100th birthday party.

Lisa White met Sandy in the late nineteen eighties through the public use and education component of the agreement she had hammered out with the state after the 1978 transfer of the island. By this time, her money drying up, her frustration with what the state was not doing around limiting hunting and maintaining roads, Sandy had dropped Genesis and the original Ossabaw Island Foundation. But she still wanted to be sure students from colleges, particularly Shorter University, high schools and environmental groups, could have the chance to visit Ossabaw on day trips.

"I had gone with a group from the Georgia Historical Society," said Lisa, who at the time was president of the Georgia Historical Society board of directors, "when I saw her walk through the arches in the clearing to her property." In her day job White is an attorney with the U.S. Army Corps of Engineers.

"After that I helped her organize the groups until the early nineties when her old private foundation, a 501(c)(4), became a nonprofit 501(c)(3)," she said. "But she wanted to be sure these same groups would keep coming."

For many people at that time Sandy was hard to deal with. They said she was unreasonable. She was prickly. She was impatient. Lisa saw something else. She saw the entire package. She reveled in Sandy's humor, her own brand of logic, her intelligence.

"She's just so curious," Lisa said. "She'll hear something and say, 'tell me about that.' She read Time magazine for years. She kept current."

Somewhere along the line Lisa recruited her friend, Louisa Abbot, to be her co-advocate. For twelve years, the two have managed monthly visits. They go on picnics, take drives, accompany Sandy on various hospital forays and take her into their homes on holidays.

"That was twelve years ago when Lisa took me out there," said Louisa, a Chatham County Superior Court Judge from the Eastern Judicial Circuit. "I was terrified to meet her. But truly, she made me feel like a big person."

Clearly it's a mutual admiration society, for humor, for humanity.

"Do you need ice?" I once heard Lisa ask Sandy before leaving her room.

"In elegant sufficiency," Sandy answered in two seconds flat, as if she were waiting for an excuse to string those three words together.

During their early visits Lisa and Louisa would sit on the stairs and listen to Sandy talk to groups that Jim Bitler brought to the island.

To me, Sandy would say about Louisa: "Can you imagine a judge making up my bed?"

There is trust between them.

"She utterly loved it being with those folks," Lisa said. "She'd hold forth in the living room in cutoffs and Keds. She could hold them spellbound for hours. She imbued them with a sense of value of wilderness."

"She's always been interested in one thing—the next big idea," said Louisa. "Always has been. She truly believes that there can be a new idea, something that can save the world. She believes that. I do too. She gets angry, like with the DNR, but she gets past it. She loves people as individuals but not as humanity.

"She didn't get to go to college but she's smarter than anyone around her. She still is. She got arrested at the Michigan State Fair for passing out Planned Parenthood literature, ala Margaret Sanger. She talked about leading a protest march, on her walker, by the clubhouse over the towers they were building. You don't meet people like that every day."

"It's quite a change from how she was raised," said Lisa, finishing Louisa's sentence and thought.

In 2003, when Sandy turned ninety, the two friends accompanied her to New York. She was one of ten people getting an award from the Garden Club of America. David Rockefeller was there.

"There we are at the Savannah Airport," said Lisa, laughing. "She's got this ancient luggage and she is wearing a ginormous belt buckle. We started walking ahead and I look back and there they are, wanding her for security."

The story continues.

"We go to check in at the hotel and she says, 'Hello, I'm Eleanor West, an esteemed medalist.' Turns out they had overbooked the hotel. Her room had a cot and some flowers. While we waited for another room we went in and saw her lying down on the cot with the flowers on her chest.

"'I'm an esteemed medalist,' she repeated, not at all impatient with the situation. Then she told us, 'I've just had the best conversation with Ruby. She's from the Dominican Republic. She's my housekeeper here. When she admired my shoes I gave them to her.'"

At the hotel Sandy, wearing a black velvet dress with short sleeves got up and "gave a most marvelous speech," said Lisa. "There were four hundred people there. There was a sign that said something like ninety years in bloom, referring to the Garden Club. She took that and ran with it. She started off thanking them for celebrating her ninetieth birthday."

Later, I found Jenny Lynn Bradley's introductory remarks about Sandy at the Georgia Historical Society,

PHOTO: JANE FISHMAN

which has fifty cubic feet of documents from the Torrey and West families. Bradley was the Garden Club of America Awards chairman.

"In one action, Mrs. West guaranteed that Ossabaw Island would never be demeaned by high rise condos or golden arches, or casinos and boardwalks, or outlet malls or tee shirt shops. Tonight we salute Eleanor Torrey West, a woman who gave up a fortune to save the island she loved, a woman who for the past half-century has devoted her life to keeping the island preserved safe from the predators of mercenary development."

None of that fancy-schmancy stuff in New York meant Sandy wasn't up for some hijinks whenever she got off the island. Lisa remembers the time she drove Sandy into the Greenwich cemetery where she and her family had lived before a fire destroyed the house.

"She hadn't been there for years," Lisa said. "She saw that the fountain was still there. Then she saw a piece of iron, maybe from an old fence, and said, 'Stop the car. I have to have some of that.' I said, 'Oh, Lordy, we're going to get arrested.' Then she said, 'But it's mine!'"

The stories continued.

"Remember the time Roger drove her and some friends to Grosse Pointe?" Louisa said.

Without answering—the cultural contrast evident—Lisa became a bit wistful thinking of "the time I saw the two of them in the kitchen on Ossabaw doing the two-step to Waylon Jennings."

Not exactly the same as dancing with Johnny Mercer at some cotillion. People change. Times change.

We paused, trying to imagine the scene: dependable Roger, always up for a horse ride with Sandy, formerly in charge of the cattle on Ossabaw, the man Sandy called "John Wayne with a brain," and Sandy, the former socialite, the debutante, the patrician.

Then Lisa had another memory. "Remember the time she had that hernia episode and they had to call an ambulance in the middle of the night to meet her at the Vernon View dock? The ambulance driver said, 'You look familiar.' Then he remembered. He used to be her exterminator inspector on the island. He'd be doing work outside her window and she'd be throwing food to her horses and pigs so of course they all started running toward him, which kind of startled him. That's when he figured it out and said, 'Oh no, not you.'"

Again, finishing one another's sentences, Lisa said, "We went to the hospital, that Sunday night, and people were coming in to introduce themselves to her and in the middle of all this drama she turned to us and said, 'I love this place.'"

"In spite of all her issues, she's resilient," Lisa said. "There was the broken arm or maybe it was the time her stomach was pressed against her chest and she had to have heroic surgery. We took turns visiting at St. Joseph's. I remember she wanted me to take the cross off the wall and put it on her chest when the priest would give the morning prayer over the P.A."

"Remember the time at three a.m. when we were bringing her to your house?" Louisa said to Lisa. "We were laughing so much in the car it looked like we were drunk. We put her in Lisa's bed and said, 'Now don't get up.' Lisa camped out by the door. At eight a.m. she walked to the door. I think she was reaching for the phone. She liked to say 'I've been telephoning, lovie.'"

Louisa came over and got in bed with her so Lisa could get ready for work. "That's when she said, 'I'm hanging by a thread watching you.' Lisa was putting on her moisturizer."

"She's a remarkable poet and storyteller," Louisa said. "Justin did a collection of her writings. One poem was about Clifford walking with Justin on his shoulder. Her kids called them 'popcorn stories.' She'd put the kids in the stories. They'd beg her for the stories. I begged her to let them be published. She loved it when I saw they were wonderful. I had her sign a bunch of the Maria Bosomworth books to everyone in my family."

To Lisa, who sometimes calls her Toady, it's Sandy's "unending curiosity and wonderment, her joi de vivre." That's what makes her keep coming back for more. "It's her dogged determination to figure for what she believes is just. Her childlike playfulness and spirit."

"I adore her," said Louisa. "Her sensibility must have been born in her. I've had conversations with her I've never had with anyone about what it's like to be a person. She has an adamant sense of wanting to live very fully. It embraces everything. Humanity disappoints her but she wants to engage individual people. It's been a real ride."

Chapter Fifteen

Sandy and Betsy

For many years Savannah artist Betsy Cain organized artists' retreats on Ossabaw Island. Awesome Ossabaw, she would call it. She would carve out a time with the Ossabaw Island Foundation, negotiate with the on-island coordinator and arrange transportation to the island. The group would bring its own food and stay in the clubhouse. If they donated a piece of art to the annual Pig Roast, they would be allowed to attend the fundraiser free of charge.

Betsy wrote the following essay for the Ossabaw Island Foundation newsletter:

Artists belong on Ossabaw Island. It is written.

It was written large in the minds of Sandy and Clifford West when they initiated the Ossabaw Island Project, inviting artists of all stripes to Ossabaw to 'experience' the island that they owned with Sandy's family. It was a visionary experiment that was shaped by the experiment itself, echoing and recognizing the creative process.

And it continued, branching out onto the Genesis Project, written now as another creative legacy for this remarkable island.

It continues today with the Foundation's Visiting Artist Program and I have been a beneficiary of this exchange

*D*on't you just love people who mark time by when Lucky the pig was alive?

Betsy and Sandy make art together.

for many years. I also work on behalf of the Foundation to bring artists to Ossabaw, an effort that brings me great pleasure. I say to these artists, 'Now, Ossabaw is yours. It will inhabit you.'

What happens when artists come to Ossabaw? Space and time become altered, perceptions stretch into the vastness of the vistas on Willows Road, sharpen under the dripping canopy of the maritime forest and move with the tidal flux and flow on South Beach. As Sandy West says, "There is room for thought here."

Visual thought is different. It is not logical thinking. It is awareness. What I have found on Ossabaw Island is a deep echo of the totality of life. I experience a prescient feeling that I know this place, despite the continual sense of discovery. This feeling resides in a collective memory of landscape as it was, as it has always been. It is almost inexplicable. There is a pulse of the unknown on this island, ripe territory for the creative soul. Ossabaw offers the strata of history continued with dense visual and audible experience. It invades my painting as a palpable energy. I take Ossabaw with me into the studio.

And it is written. Artists belong on Ossabaw.

Betsy met Sandy through Gordon Varnedoe.

"He brought me over to the island. It was a trade. Larry Gray, an artist friend of mine in Savannah, had given me a painting of his. After that he had had an open house and Gordon and (his wife) Catherine fell in love with the same painting he gave me. Gordon asked 'What do we have to do to get this painting?' I didn't hesitate. I said you can take me to Ossabaw to meet Mrs. West. She met us at the dock. Lucky, the pig, was still alive so it must have been 1995." (Betsy was telling this story in front of Sandy. When she got to the part about the pig, Sandy interrupted to say, "Don't you just love people who mark time by when Lucky the pig was alive?")

"Sandy drove us around the island. She had her Jeep. We had lunch in the patio. We brought a picnic. Joan (Cobitz) and Catherine (Varnedoe) came. I didn't get back until the first Pig Roast twelve years ago."

These days Betsy is part of a crew to "look after Sandy." To Betsy, who spends a couple days a week on Ossabaw, "there is no better window in the world to stand in front of to wash dishes." She has spent Thanksgiving, Christmas and New Year's with Sandy.

Somewhere around the summer of 2013, Betsy started painting with Sandy. A few years earlier I had discovered a cache of paintings Sandy had done when she lived in Bloomfield Hills, Michigan. They were very good. Two of her oil paintings hang in the hall of her house. The night we looked through her portfolio, when she was getting into bed, she turned to me and said, "I think my future is bright."

During one visit Sandy told me that on every birthday she would find a road no one used—or a deserted paddock—where she would sit by herself and paint a picture.

When I told Betsy about her stack of paintings, she hit the ground running and started painting with Sandy. The two had discovered a shared interest. With Sandy's consent, two paintings were auctioned off at the 2013 Pig Roast. In the end, they raised $3,000.

When Nancy Marshall and her husband, John McWilliams, old friends of Sandy's and artists themselves, visited they got to see Sandy painting with Betsy.

"She (Sandy) wanted me to see the paintings," Nancy said. "It was the neatest thing to watch them together. There was Sandy painting on her breakfast tray and Betsy getting her scissors out, finding brushes, getting her water. Then Betsy got in bed next to her and said, 'You go first.' She did a line and then Betsy did one. Sandy was very focused. An hour later they were still working on the same painting." It sounded to me like a form of the exquisite corpse where surrealists would finish one another's words or images.

Sandy and Betsy have a lively good time together. There is little they don't talk about.

Sandy to Betsy: "You didn't bite you nails?"

Betsy: "No."

Sandy: "You missed a lot."

Lately, Betsy has been painting Sandy's fingernails and toenails, different colors for different seasons. For Thanksgiving, every other nail was blue and green. For Christmas, they alternated silver and red, for New Year's, solid gold. For Valentine's Day, she got a coat of hot pink.

In early December, I got in bed with the two artists and we all took turns painting. That's when Sandy told us, "You know, lately I've been fascinated by tree bark.

"In the south they're so very, very different," she said. "I just think it would be great to make something out of them. Wouldn't it be wonderful to make a painting and put it on a mat in a certain way? Like an etching."

"It'd be hard to paint," Betsy said. "But you could do it," Sandy said. "We could collect some bark," Betsy said. "Why don't we do that tomorrow?"

Sandy said. "That would be divine. Remember the road we found that didn't make any sense? Let's try it."

So the next day the three of us pile into the Jeep and go looking for bark. When we see a tree with an interesting texture—a sabal palm, a pecan, a magnolia—we stop, get out, take a few samples, hug the tree for balance, throw our head back and look straight up into the branches. It is an Ossabaw moment, one of those times that lodge in your head and won't go away. We're on an island. We see pigs rooting around, looking for something to eat. They're ten feet away. We stand still hoping to watch them longer. But they hear us. They stop, confused, or are they curious? They've felt our presence. Then they dart away and make a break for safer ground.

Sandy is back to business.

"Nobody really looks at bark," she said.

Except for us. We were looking at bark.

Chapter Sixteen

Sandy and Friends

It's interesting that everyone who knows Sandy seems to remember the exact time and place where they met. For Gordon Varnedoe, it was when he was a kid. Varnedoe comes from a long lineage of Savannahians. One grandfather, Gordon Saussy, was mayor of the city, the other grandfather, John Kirk Train, was a doctor. His mother, Lilla Train, was the first female member of the board of education before she became board president.

"I was sixteen," started Gordon. "My girlfriend at the time—Anne Mercer, Johnny Mercer's niece—and I loved to go boating. I had a boat at Vernon View dock, four houses down from where Anne grew up. We liked to go to Wassaw, another barrier island off Georgia. One day we went to Ossabaw, you know, just two kids. We thought Sandy would run us off. We were trespassing, but as you know there are no 'No trespassing' signs on Ossabaw. But she welcomed us—maybe it was 1954? It turns out Sandy had got drinks from my father at the Oglethorpe Club when she was underage. She invited us in. We had iced tea.

"I was amazed at when Sandy got older, her spirit, well, you talk about the unsinkable Molly Brown, that's Sandy. Determination, that's what kept her going.

"She's not angry. She laughs a lot. She's enchanting. If she'd told us to stand on our heads we would have. It's been a long and wonderful association. I treasure it. Five years ago at one of her birthday celebrations I got down on my knees and asked her to marry me. Lisa White will be the wedding planner. Ask her."

Let's face it; it's hard not to like Sandy.

Roger Parker, Sandy, and Richard Boaen at the 2012 Pig Roast.

Technically, Zelda Tenenbaum met the island before she met Sandy. When Lee Adler, Savannah's historic preservation guru, was trying to form a non-profit 501(c)(3) foundation for Ossabaw, he recruited Tenenbaum, a consultant, for her skills in bringing groups together. This was after the state had assumed management of the island. Adler and others were replacing Sandy's foundation—never a nonprofit—with something more legitimate.

"People kept telling me she was negative," Zelda said. "They warned me, 'Oh, she's going to tell you these stories, she's going to complain and say she was the victim of the DNR.' She did say those things, but she was right. The DNR wasn't doing anything."

Sandy, Zelda said, was a "true flower child. Maybe the original flower child. There's a part of her that's new age spiritual. Life had to catch up with her. She reminds me of Katie Lee, who saved Glen Canyon in Telluride, Colorado. They flooded it for a dam. Katie still fights to have it undone. She's over one hundred years old. They both have the spirit, the passion, and the indomitable drive to fight for what they believe.

"We kept listening to Sandy and in the end much of what she was saying was true. All the state was doing was organizing hunts and doing some

Sandy and Gordon.

maintenance. Eventually we asked what if they did things like road maintenance and we developed programs. We convinced them if they didn't want to do the education end, we could.

"Sandy is a warrior. Hers was a story of plight. She was a model of the warrior who is passionate and won't let go. She knows people. She reads people. She looks after humanity. She sees the bigger picture. She's a storyteller. She's a cultural anthropologist social worker and she has a good heart. She's always concerned. That's part of her. She asks how people are doing. She's a listener."

And then there's Leigh Goff, a marketer and conference organizer from Atlanta. She met Sandy through her friend, Lisa White, four years ago, but such was the connection with this near-octogenarian, Leigh decided to step in and organize a doozy of a celebration for Sandy's ninety-ninth birthday. With Lisa's help she stamped and addressed ninety-nine envelopes to Sandy West and enclosed each envelope with cards that read, "To celebrate your 99th birthday, I'm going to…"

"Those letters ended up being one of the best presents I've ever given myself," Leigh said, "because I happened to be there when Sandy read some of them. You know how she acts, like the meal she's eating right now is 'The Best Food' she's ever had? Same way with those letters. The fact that friends and strangers took time to write her seemed to thrill her. Patty Maddox, a portrait artist from Cairo, Georgia, wrote telling us all about her husband, a retired veterinarian, and his love of animals. Art and animals all in one letter! They've never met but Sandy acted like Patty was her long lost best friend forever.

"I am not an artist so couldn't figure out a legitimate way to visit. Rose Lane Leavell organized an artist trip in November of 2011 and I talked my way in by being the COOK for the group. They let me out of the kitchen long enough to meet Sandy during that first visit. I've been back several times with Lisa since then."

Janie and Peter Brodhead met Sandy when they opened their Savannah store, Brighter Day Natural Foods, in 1978. "She was one of our first customers," Janie said. "We were twenty-four, Sandy was sixty-three. We thought she was the 'hippest old person' we had ever met."

"We had no idea anyone that old could be that hip," Peter said. "She came to my herb- and jelly-making class. We made ointments and cough syrups. She found us pretty quickly."

"She was a real networker," Janie said. "She'd bring artists into the store. Then there was this self-proclaimed herbalist from Genesis who was quite a character. When we went to Ossabaw for her one-hundredth birthday I mentioned this woman and Sandy remembered her. She said, 'Such a rascal.' Imagine opening your island to people. Now, from my perspective I think what it would be like to open my house to so many people. She commands a space in a great way. You would just drop everything when she came in the store.

"The conversation is never about Sandy West. She's interested in other people. She'll say, 'How are the kids?' She's always so interested in everything. You just don't meet people like this. She's just so accepting, so interested, so curious about other people. She doesn't talk about herself so much. She never pulls the wealthy woman card. She's very honestly who she is. There's no pretension. At the store she'd just start talking to customers in the aisle. "She's always had interesting people around her. She called the store once and said, 'I just want to tell you and Peter you need to slow down and enjoy life more.'

"She's such an inspiration as a woman watching someone age. It makes you wonder what makes this old person different than the old people we know. I think it's that she's playful. She hung out with people who were young. When you see her, it's a party. She's like looking into the future. She told us at her one-hundredth party, 'I'm glad I'm not you. I don't have to deal with all you deal with.' That was such a sweet party.

"You know, I realized we don't know Sandy that well, but every time you're around her she makes you feel like she knows you."

Amanda Wrona Meadows met Sandy when she married Andy Meadows, who works for the Georgia Department of Natural Resources. Amanda has a doctorate in marine science and works for The Nature Conservancy in global marine programs.

"Here I was a young scientist thinking science would cure everything," Amanda said. "But time after time it was Sandy who made me think of the really big issues. I'd get back from a conference on, say, the loss of shortnose sturgeon, where all the discussion was about measuring and tracking them, and Sandy would say, 'Well, did you tell them what the real problem is? That there are too many people in the world? That they are straining our resources?' And she was right. That was the elephant in the room that no one wanted to address."

The most successful conference Amanda ever attended was on Ossabaw.

"I brought a team of scientists from all over the world to her house, with Sandy's permission, of course. It was a work/planning retreat to save the world's oceans. We met in her dining room and had breakout sessions in the rest of the house. To this day people are still talking about it. There was something about not having TV or cell phones, about not being able to go to town when the meeting was over. We talked about problems. We took a field trip piled in trucks to the beach. We weren't in some stupid conference room, sterile environment. It was magical."

Chapter Seventeen

Will You Be in My Army?

As her longtime confidant, close friend and fellow conspirator, John "Crawfish" Crawford knows as much about Sandy West's conflicting views on the relationship between Ossabaw Island and technology—or modern science, as Sandy may say—as anyone. Crawford has had Sandy's ear, heart and confidence for forty years, ever since he and others started Wilderness Southeast in 1973. Wilderness Southeast is a non-profit organization geared toward nature tours. Sandy, Crawford says, "is no different than the rest of us who struggle to find the right and comfortable place in our lives for technology, relevant information and connectivity."

It's complicated.

"For starters, she loves her phone," he says, as anyone who visits her will know. The large landline phone that broadcasts the number, who is behind that number, the date, the time, propped near her in bed, is a lifeline to friends and family. She uses it daily and intelligently.

"She's resigned to her computer, too," Crawford said, "though not as much now. People forget that for the longest time radio contact was all she and anyone else on the island had. Other people could listen in and it wasn't as handy."

Before that there was a generator.

"It ran twenty-four hours a day. It was loud. They had to haul diesel fuel over to run it."

I don't think they know that the island is there because of her far-sightedness.

Before Georgia Power ran a power line inside a fiber optic line from the north end of Skidaway Island under the river and the marsh, Sandy probably never knew what real uninterrupted quiet sounded like. "It sounds contradictory and in some ways it is," Crawford said.

Now eagles sit on the old phone lines, he added, not without irony.

Now there is technology.

Now, as part of the Ossabaw Barrier Island Observatory, established in 2008 and 2009, way after Sandy's sole ownership of the island, there is a relationship between the state of Georgia, Armstrong Atlantic State University, a few science communities in the state and those who are interested in environmental data.

Now there are sensors, video cameras, radio transmitters, solar panels with backup batteries, cable lines and towers beaming back information to the mainland about geological shifts, weather changes and water quality in groundwater wells and surface wells. From this data graduate students can test the salinity of the water or the temperature of the chemicals in the wells.

"It's all pretty dry information," Crawford said.

But the main sticking point for Sandy?

Crawford hesitated before he continued. We were sitting under the boughs of a spreading live oak in front of Crawford's Isle of Hope home. The afternoon was quiet. A neighbor was riding his bike back and forth at a steady pace. Bluebirds darted in and out of a homemade birdhouse. A stray cat that someone had probably dropped off was testing Crawford's patience. But Crawford is a calm man. He knows Sandy, but he knows the world, too.

"The main sticking point?" he repeated.

At this point Crawford could have put himself in Sandy's shoes and spoken of a lot of things important to her—and maybe to him—things that are disappearing because of technology. The loss of mystery. The loss of darkness. The loss of the invisible. The loss of free, uninterrupted time. The loss of silence. With cell phones we no longer lose our way, either in books or woods. We choose not to rely on serendipitous happenings, on the kindness of strangers. Our intuition is minimized and dulled. We are, in the end, too connected, too available to distraction. Our gaze has lowered.

Instead, Crawford spoke of the towers. "The towers and their placement," he said. "That's the first thing she talked to me about the day of the Pig Roast in October—the loss of the beautiful vista."

Sandy saw the monitoring device on Willows Road for the first time when someone was taking her for a ride. "She told me she looked at it and said, 'What the hell?'" said Crawford. "But it was later, when she was on a boat, that she saw one of the two one-hundred-foot towers sticking up.

"I mean, picture it," he said. "Up until then the tallest thing had always been a pine tree. Without too much thought a couple of scientists from the Skidaway Institute, a chemist and geologist, maybe not aware of the aesthetics, put these things on the same platform where people like to sit and paint and fish.

"In all fairness," Crawford said, "the people who put up the transmitter did not get proper directions. What I would have said if anyone had asked me was to place them hidden, out of sight."

Then he took a breath. He sighed and said, "I don't think they know that the island is there because of her far-sightedness."

But by the time of the millennium that type of isolation was history. For that to happen, people visiting the island would have to empty their pockets of phones and dump them on the table at the outset, not unlike gunslingers leaving their weapons at the door, or stashing them in their rooms. The genie was out of the bottle. Sandy, in her mid-nineties, had a lot of adjusting to do. She was getting accustomed to the new Ossabaw Island Foundation, the nonprofit body that was formed after the state took over the island, but her personal money was running out. People at the state were tired of hearing from her. Physically, she was dealing with balance problems, a wonky knee and lack of mobility. And she was having trouble realizing she was no longer in charge. She could still follow the dots, but it dawned on her she didn't like what she was seeing.

Wild pig.

So she started to work the phones. She needed allies. She needed ears. She needed the backing of the "big punkins," people who cared about keeping Ossabaw wild, people like herself who could question the aesthetics of placing two one-hundred-foot towers on the island's main road.

And with good reason.

For years Ossabaw represented a place to get away from phone calls, whether you were there as a guest of Sandy's parents, a member of Sandy and Clifford's Ossabaw Island Project, or a participant in the Genesis Project. It was a place to disconnect. It was where you went to feel your shoulders drop a few inches, where you didn't have to stay alert to the ring of a telephone, the ping of a text message or the buzz of an email. You knew you couldn't go online to mail a sudden thought or to see if someone had returned a text message. So you didn't try. Your options were limited to your imagination, your senses, your ability to discover, your inventiveness. A boat represented your only connection to the mainland and even that had to coordinate with the tides, with available drivers. It's why people used to go to remote islands—to let new thoughts, new feelings, new emotions make themselves known.

Make no mistake. The island is remote. One day I was staying at the house after Sandy had had a hernia operation. I was one of a half dozen people who would go over to keep her company, to help out and to get a little bit of Ossabawonderful love ourselves. Before this she had a few nurses from the mainland who were unaccustomed to island life.

"The first one asked where the curtains were," Sandy said of a caretaker. "Can you imagine? Then she wondered where the television was."

Not that I wasn't sometimes freaked out in the house. I was. There are too many doors to count. They can't all be locked. There are too many windows. They can't be locked either. Often there was no one else on the island. That takes getting used to.

So do other things. During a visit last year I started to get a little worried about a bite on my neck that was starting to redden.

"I think it's a tick bite, or several," I told Sandy, thinking about a couple cases of Lyme disease I had read about. "I spent about forty minutes trying to get the head of the tick out."

Sandy took her magnifying glasses—always nearby—and looked closely. Then she reached into the dresser next to her bed and handed me some tea tree oil, an extract from the melaleuca plant, maybe something Queenie taught her.

"Try this, lovie," she said. "I wouldn't worry about him. He's dead as a smelt. You'll be fine."

And then, forgetting my bites, she launched into one of her favorite subjects. "If we could get beyond the universe and forget everything we knew we could save the world," she said. "That's the way the wheel came about. One day it wasn't there. Then it was. The same thing with fire. We only use ten percent of our brain. The other ninety we're afraid of. We're afraid of the unknown. The unknown can save us. The man who invented the wheel wasn't that intelligent, you know."

For people to think Sandy does not want to share the island with the outside world is wrong, Crawford said. She does. If she doesn't want it overrun with backpackers, she also doesn't want it to sit like some museum. She doesn't want it to exist only for hunters or people of privilege.

"She doesn't want someone in Atlanta, some kid in school, maybe, sitting in a classroom and seeing alligators online and thinking they have had the Ossabaw experience," Crawford said. "That is not the same thing. That would be Disneyfying the island. This is a rare place. We take many school groups and teach workshops and go turtling at night. They experience the effect of the high and low tides, the darkness. That can't happen online."

More than once Sandy has quoted to me from one of her favorite books, *Last Child in the Woods: Saving our Children from Nature-Deficit Disorder,* by Richard Louv.

"Listen to this," she said once, picking up the book she was reading before going to bed and going to a section she had marked. "It's a note from a fourth-grader in San Diego. 'I like to play indoors better because that's where all the electrical outlets are.' Can you imagine?"

Then, surrounded by books, old favorites and new releases people continue to send her, she looked down at the beautiful coastal cover of another book, another new gift, Charles Seabrook's *The World of the Salt Marsh,* and said, "It just makes me weep. Anything beautiful that hasn't been made by man, they can't leave their hands off it."

Betsy Cain told me this one day: "I used to argue the benefits of technology with her years ago, but I think I have come over to her side."

Another time more recently, with just as much anger and wit and perspicacity, Sandy said, "With all this technology (cell phones) people are becoming more like machines." Then, pausing for dramatic effect, as she, a natural storyteller can do, she continued. "Maybe we should let that happen. Then we can just take their batteries.

Sandy at her mirror.

It's easier than bumping them off."

Sandy tries to address many of these issues at the annual Pig Roast, where she has a live and eager audience who want to see the island, the house and Sandy herself. She rarely disappoints. By now her message is pretty simple, pretty clear. Give yourself the gift of quiet, she says. Give yourself room to let a new idea appear. She speaks off the cuff. She speaks from the heart. "Human beings have a terrible time keeping their hands off things," she says.

Before the trouble with technology, there was hunting. That was a big issue after she sold—or gifted, as some people say—Ossabaw to the state.

"She does not like hunting for recreation," said Crawford. "The thing is the wildlife management division of the DNR manages the island and hunting is their main focus. Sandy was so afraid they'd turn it into a hunting preserve, like it used to be. They argued it was necessary to keep the deer and wild hog populations down—and it was; she agreed to that—but she argued against the turkey and duck hunts. There weren't many turkeys and ducks because they were migratory. She was successful. In the end under the agreement, no small game or duck hunted for recreational purposes was allowed. This was very important to Sandy."

She's also big on the activity of listening.

"I have found the main thing that should be talked about is listening for a length of time," she said, "especially when you're alone and no one is talking to you."

At another Pig Roast gathering Sandy told her group a story about Elizabeth DuBose, director of the "new" Ossabaw Island Foundation. Elizabeth had brought some expert to the island to try to figure out what to do with the house.

"The first thing I noticed on his vita?" Sandy told the crowd. "It said, 'He's a listener.' Isn't that blessed? I've had time when no one is talking to me or playing music, just silence and I've heard the darndest things."

Another time Sandy said, "Thank you for being an army. I wish I could hug every bloody one of you. You can ride a horse forty miles on this island and not see the same thing. We need to keep it that way. My blessed Elizabeth (DuBose) and Paul (Pressly) are here but they could slip under a bus. Will you watch with me? I'm going to croak pretty soon. This kind of thing, technology, is sneaky. It's the sneakiest thing I ever looked at. Bless you for coming."

Crawford is thoughtful when considering Sandy.

"Remember what she said at the pig roast a few years ago?"

And then, paraphrasing, Crawford remembered, "She said, 'You know what the world is like, with machines and all. I need to enlist you as my constabularies. Will you watch with me? Will you be in my army?'"

Chapter Eighteen

Sandy and her Blessed People

If Sandy West wasn't calling the people she loved "blessed," it was one or another of the animals on the island. In one of Sandy's earlier periods with her "blessed people," in this case the four-leggeds, she hosted the Yerkes Primate Projects. With her permission, in 1972, the Yerkes Primate Research Center at Emory University released one male and three female chimpanzees on Bear Island on the north end of Ossabaw. The National Institutes of Health funded this experiment.

"Yerkes was looking for a way to produce chimps to see if they would breed in a free roaming setting," Sandy said. "In captivity young were raised with surrogate 'towels' which were supposed to replace (mothers).

"Tigs (the female) and Jaki (the male) had a baby we called Sandy. What we saw was, she simply dragged the baby around like a doll/rag since Jaki was brought up as a 'towel-mothered' captive.

"We contacted Yerkes to inform them that Sandy had been born. Since Jaki didn't know what or how to deal with the infant, I was permitted to go to the site and was given Sandy, the baby. I carried her in my arms to the house. Project members watched me cradling a baby quietly into the main house. Rumors abounded that Mrs. West had a baby.

"The baby chimp howled terribly in my room. I slipped my finger in its mouth. It was quiet, then noisy. I was told not to feed it as the Yerkes' vets had formulas and since he was the first 'free ranging chimp' born in

I went to every man on the island and asked, "Would you rather be sold or castrated?" They didn't want either one.

North America. Anyway, we waited until the Yerkes vet came to my room. He picked up the baby by the ankles and popped it on the rump (I guess) and said quiet! "The baby chimp went quiet. The vet said, 'I'm sorry, I forgot to tell you how to quiet one down.' Within a couple of years the baby chimp died."

Unlike the pigs, which were brought over by the Spanish as ballast and considered an element of cultural history, the introduction of donkeys was a mistake, said Sandy.

"Oh, it was a terrible sin I committed bringing them here," she said. "They're quite dear. They're Sicilians. Some called them Christian donkeys because of a dark cross-shaped marking down the spine and across the shoulders, but let's be sure, they are not cultural history.

"When my son Justin was ten we imported some Sicilian donkeys from Bull Island, South Carolina. We brought four donkeys back in the back seat of our mini-bus. They're so blissful. We had at the most eight. When we sold the island to the state, ten years later, there were eighty-three. They originally came from Abyssinia, the desert, in Sicily. They thrived like mad. They needed to be sold or castrated. I went to every man on the island and asked, 'Would you rather be sold or castrated?' They didn't want either one. I felt protective of them because Penn State University had been conducting studies on donkey behavior on Ossabaw for several years. Castration would ruin the research.

"Well, I was riding down the road on my horse one day and having been involved with Planned Parenthood and population control I thought why not vasectomize them. That might be the only way to manage it for animals where there are no natural predators. I called Penn State. They said if you could round up those donkeys in six weeks we'll come down. They said they would do it for free. They had already done it with racehorses. Those donkeys can run faster than a horse so it wasn't easy. Roger [Parker] and I would get up in the middle of the night and run them into a field. We filled cattle pens scattered around the island. A helicopter came in with vets who wore little green operating suits. They made us boil water and set up tables of sterile instruments. It was an outdoor operating room in Buckhead Field.

"We gave them a tranquilizer, then a shot. The folks from Penn State were here three days. All the males survived and the study went on, their behavior pretty much the same. Everyone snickered at me but people wrote from as far away as France."

Armadillos, another resident of the island, have never become one of Sandy's pets but she likes the way they co-exist with the donkeys.

For the longest time Sandy had a pet goose she called Christmas. But then he disappeared. When her son Justin and his wife Eileen ran across an "animal communicator" at some festival in Massachusetts, where they live, they bought two half-hour sessions to see if Sandy could communicate with the goose. The communicator is a type of psychic who uses telepathy to speak to one's pets. One does not have to be with the person or the animal to communicate. They also bought Sandy a phone card to cover the long distance charge.

Sandy liked the idea. So she called and asked about Christmas, the goose. She was told two people had come one night with lots of food and cages. Many animals were trapped but Christmas got away and hid under a wheelbarrow for four days. Then he got lonely and set off to find his friends.

He ended up at a place with a lot of chickens, the communicator said. For a while he stayed and put on a lot of weight. But then he was afraid he couldn't make it "home." Three years later he made it back. Christmas mentioned the place had changed. It was untidy and the lawn needed to be mowed. He said Sandy walked slower and needed a cane. Christmas slyly suggested the cane could be used to hit Toby (the beagle). He doesn't like the dog, the psychic said, because Toby chases him. He also suggested that a light by the stable would be a good idea.

Sandy wanted to know why Christmas always follows the horses. Christmas told the psychic, "He liked watching their bums go up down and side to side."

The animal communicator said she also talked to Lucky, one of Sandy's favorite pigs. He can walk again, she said, and Sandy should not worry anymore about having him put down as he didn't want to live that way anymore.

One of Sandy's favorite stories, which has appeared on many Pig Roast invitations, is the following:

One bright, crisp and heavenly morning I walked down the long back hall of my beautiful old house and started down the steps to the road. At the bottom of the steps was a ruffly black puddle. As I watched, the black puddle unfolded and became a small black piglet who in time became Paul Mitchell. He was named for the famous hairdresser who was badly needed by Paul.

Just like our beloved Lucky Pig, Paul grew up in the house and accompanied me on every adventure. You know what animals will grow up to be, what THE ANIMALS are supposed to be if humans will let them. I never tried to make Paul what I thought pigs should be. He is definitely a pig that is himself.

Toby chases an armadillo.

He dearly loves a man that works on the island called Richard. When Richard comes in the morning Paul follows his truck a mile up to my house. They immediately go under my window and Paul gives Richard's pocket a healthy snout whack. Then Richard takes his cell phone out of his pocket and sticks it under Paul's nose. Paul snorts and growls and chats until Richard removes the phone. Upstairs on my cell phone, I hear the operator say, "Message finished. It will be saved for twenty-one days."

Chapter Nineteen

Great-Grandfather Ford

If Sandy calls her mother a "heavenly creature," her father "a big brain," and Hermes her chief messenger between heaven and earth, then Captain John Baptiste Ford, her great-grandfather, would have to be considered her guiding light.

"I get goose pimples just thinking about him," she has said. "He's the most remarkable man who ever, ever was."

All this about a man she never met. But you'd never know that. The first half dozen times I heard her mention him I assumed they were close. Then I did the math. He died in 1903, ten years before Sandy was born. Then I figured out he was her great-grandfather, although she tends to call him "Grandfather Ford."

Like her father, he was not born into wealth. He did not have privilege. He did not have an easy time in this young, wide open, newly developing country. He ran away from his hardscrabble home in New Albany, Indiana to Louisville, Kentucky. He apprenticed himself to "everybody and their grandmother" he could find, according to Sandy. He'd return home with cartloads of saddles, hats or shoes or anything else he could cobble together to make a living. His mind was all over the place, Sandy said. He married young, lost the first five of his children, and then ran away again, trying to find his way. He was driven.

When he started working at a glass company—before he headed it—he sent his workers to Belgium to

If you don't see me behind every bush or every tree on this island, I have not done something right.

learn how to pour glass and make a window. Armed with information, he started a business that became the Pittsburgh Plate Glass Company, just in time to manufacture glass for the nation's first skyscrapers.

"But then he got into a big fight with someone he worked with and he just left," Sandy said, grinning as if to say she admired his spirit. "One of his sons, Emory, my grandfather, left with him. The other son, Edward, said, 'You're out of your sponge. I'm not going along with your dumb plans.' So he stayed and created Libby Owen Ford. They were the Toledo Fords. We were the Detroit Fords."

Sandy knows a lot of this from the letters Grandfather Ford left behind, many of them to his wife, Mary Bower, each one starting the same: "Dear Mrs. Ford."

"There he would be, out in the world somewhere, starting another business and there she would be, that long-suffering woman, home with the kids. I named a rowboat after Mary Bower, blessed thing. He'd write, 'I'm so sorry I'm not home. I know you are having a hard time with your arthritis. Oh, and I may not have long to live myself.'" Sandy, pausing before finishing her point, said, "Of course, then he would live twenty-five more years."

Somewhere in this topsy-turvy career of starting and leaving businesses, Grandfather Ford went bankrupt and had to sell everything.

"All day long he and Mary Bower sat up in the top floor of their house and watched everything they owned be sold at auction," Sandy said. "At the end of the day they walked away from the house hand in hand, not knowing where they would be living. Before long they saw all the people in the town waiting for them. Turns out the town had bought the house, bought all their things and given them back to him and his wife. Isn't that blessed?"

He had that kind of effect on people, Sandy said. When one of his plants in Ford City, Pennsylvania—a town named after him—was up and running and employing a huge workforce, "the workers loved him so much they built a statue of him facing the factory." This was in the 1890s, when he and the factory were still alive and well.

"When the plant closed one hundred years later, a new generation of townspeople knew Ford wouldn't have wanted to stare at a defunct factory so they turned the statue around so it could face the town instead," said Sandy.

Apocryphal? Hard to say. She believes it. She lives by it.

But here's the story that Sandy seems to like the most, the one that seems to give her most pause when thinking of Ford.

"At eighty-seven, when you would think he was well off financially, Grandfather Ford was riding on a train—I'm not sure where he was going—dressed in a tall silk hat and silk coat because that's what he wore when he traveled, when he saw some land near Wyandotte, Michigan along the Detroit River. He looked out and thought there might be something there that would help him produce soda ash, a necessary ingredient to make glass, a business he still had his hands in, by the way. He thought, 'I don't know why I shouldn't buy this.' So he pulled the train's emergency brake cord lever to stop the train.

"Then he got out and bought the land."

When I called the Wyandotte Historical Society to ask about this someone told me Ford's instincts were right, that the strata of pure salt under the site would be what he needed to produce soda ash, a major ingredient in the manufacture of glass.

This, says Sandy, was the start of J.B. Ford Company Glassworks. Eventually this business consolidated with Michigan Alkali to become Wyandotte Chemicals Corporation. In 1969 it became part of BASF, now one of the world's largest chemical companies.

"Thank goodness it was sold because by this time I had become environmentally conscious," Sandy said. "I was glad not to have it in the family, but I was also glad to collect the big green to do what I can with Ossabaw. But can you believe that man? Grandfather Ford is very much a part of me."

Today, a portrait of Grandfather Ford and his faithful, capable wife hangs in the house. They are wearing black. They look serious, determined.

Sandy told me she looks at that picture and thinks about Archimedes, a Greek mathematician and inventor.

"Archimedes said if he could sit on the edge of the universe and forget everything that he ever knew, he might have an idea that could save us. That is sort of what I have been doing lately."

Once I asked her how she wanted to be remembered.

"As someone wanting to try to help people to see," she said. "They are certainly on the wrong track. Religion has a lot to do with it but not for the reason you think. Not one person in religion mentions laughter. Betty Pool thinks the way Jesus got a crowd was through laughter. Guests wrote they come to Ossabaw just to hear laughter. I bet Jesus was funny. You never think about anyone around him being funny."

Great-grandfather Ford.

But then she was back to Grandfather Ford.

"Every time I see him I think he is hammering and yammering at me," she said. "I'm the only one in the family who took a chance. I think he quite likes me, but I wish he'd leave me alone and give me a little peace and quiet. But you know he won't. I have to keep doing these terrible things. Even when I don't want to keep going he picks me up, shakes me and makes me. I've inherited his ghost, unfortunately."

Then she stopped to laugh because she knew and I knew she was only half serious.

"People ought to be able to rest now and then, don't you think? But there's Grandfather telling me to get off that sand dune and get to work. He is the reason Ossabaw is here."

I keep thinking what Sandy said to Jim Bitler, as recorded in his spiral notebook.

"Once I told her I didn't know what I would do when she was gone," wrote Jim. "Without missing a beat, she looked right at me and said, 'If you don't see me behind every bush or every tree on this island, I have not done something right.'"

I don't think there's anything to worry about.

In the same way the people of Ford City, Indiana have a statue of John Baptiste Ford facing the river, I'm guessing there will be a vision of Eleanor "Sandy" Torrey West behind every palmetto, in the path of every great blue heron, on the wide expanse of each high tide rolling into Ossabaw. She'll be there—with a story, a pop-in idea, a new-fangled word. We just may have to sit very still and be very quiet to hear it.

Acknowledgments

The more I started writing about Ossabaw Island's Sandy West the more I realized how many holes the book would contain. Some friends who read it first asked, "But what about her husbands? What about her money? What about her children?" A few asked, "But what are her shortcomings? Everyone's got shortcomings." Someone else said it read like a "puff piece," a feature story that ignores evidence to the contrary, anathema in journalism. I had to think about all that. These were smart people asking smart questions. And then I decided this wasn't a biography. This wasn't an investigative piece of journalism. This wasn't a "let's look at both sides" kind of book.

This was a "let's look at Sandy" book. Maybe, now that I read it again, it is—horrors!—a puff piece. But is that so horrible? She's outspoken. She's opinionated. She's assertive. She's analog. And yes, sometimes she's pig-headed. To me, those are good qualities. But that's me.

In the end I had to go with what I thought was most relevant and most interesting. I hope the book fills some gaps. I hope her story, her style, her passion works to inspire people to fight for what they believe in, to pick up their eyes from their smartphones long enough to look around at the world. Her style is analog. She still makes lists. She still sends thank-you notes, handwritten and legible. She still talks to people one-on-one. No faceless "likes" for her on a Facebook page.

While the words, the observations, the memories, the drawings and the interpretations are mine, a project like this doesn't happen in a vacuum. Ossabaw Island Foundation director Elizabeth DuBose—whose organization does a terrific job—has been most generous sharing what she knows, including seven CDs of interviews with Sandy that go way back through the decades. The problem there is we don't know who is doing the interviewing or when the interviews were conducted. But they were classic Sandy—curious, thoughtful, funny, sometimes irreverent and always reaching for some truth, maybe, just maybe, stretching a truth for the sake of a good story. I can't fault her there. A good story goes a long way.

Frida and flowers in the sink.

I've read some exceptional books about Ossabaw, namely *Ossabaw, Evocations of an Island*, by Jack Leigh, James Kilgo and Alan Campbell, and *Images of America, Ossabaw Island*, by Ann Foskey. And if anyone has ever heard Paul Pressly speak about Ossabaw know that you're listening to a master historian.

With Sandy's permission I have reproduced photographs from her home to help the story along. When I could, I have credited the photographer.

Along the way, I had great help from Lisa White and Louisa Abbot, constant and attentive friends of

Sandy's, who laugh a lot together; Betsy Cain, another long-term Ossabaw admirer who has introduced so many artists to the island, and to the "madam," one of our favorite names for Sandy; from photographer David Kaminsky, the very patient and very talented Tom Greensfelder, and good friends and good readers Daniel Snyder, Mary Landers and Gene Downs.

   Finally, a big thanks to Susan Earl who generously offered the great early photographs of Sandy. In one, she is standing ramrod straight and with great purpose broadcasting seeds in a newly plowed garden, probably at the Genesis Project; in another she is leaning back on the dunes, laughing to beat the band while putting on a shoe. The photographs were taken by John Earl, Susan's late husband, the fine photographer who spent so much time on Ossabaw; and digitized by their daughter, Emily Earl, a pretty good photographer herself. Jim Bitler's notebooks were a gift from the Foundation and Bitler's partner, Jack Sinopolis. The background to the cover design, an encaustic painting of Ossabaw, and many other photographs, were taken by artist Carmela Aliffi, who is for me, a constant source of good humor, good sense and good food.